Getting Started in Computing for the Older Generation

Jim Gatenby

BERNARD BABANI (publishing) LTD
The Grampians
Shepherds Bush Road
London W6 7NF
England

www.babanibooks.com

IT/PC

Please Note

© 2009 BERNARD BABANI (publishing) LTD

First Published – June 2009

British Library Cataloguing in Publication Data:

A catalogue record for this book is available from the British Library

ISBN 978-0-85934-704-4

Cover Design by Gregor Arthur

Printed and bound in Great Britain for Bernard Babani (publishing) Ltd

Preface

The benefits of using your own computer can be enormous at any age, but especially so later in life. However, if you've little or no experience in this field, the idea of buying and starting to use a computer can be very daunting. This book aims to help the inexperienced user to choose a suitable computing setup for their own home so they can begin to enjoy the many new opportunities this will bring. For example, communicating with friends and family anywhere in the world using e-mail, finding the latest information on any subject and getting bargain prices from the Internet, editing and printing your own photographs or starting your own business working from home.

Computing is laden with jargon such as "gigabytes" and "dual-core processors", for example, and many of us find this off-putting. Some jargon is unavoidable and this is explained throughout the text. Chapter 9, "The Anatomy of a Computer", provides a deeper explanation of some of the more technical topics. The main components common to all computers and the associated jargon are explained; Chapter 9 is intended to be referred to when unfamiliar terms are encountered in the text.

Early chapters discuss connecting and setting up one or more computers and how to get online to the Internet using a device called a *wireless router*. The Windows operating system controls everything done by the computer and this is discussed in detail, together with Windows' help for users with special needs, etc. The installation and use of essential software such as Microsoft Office is also covered. A later chapter gives advice for maintaining your computer and preventing attack from hackers and viruses. Although this book was prepared using Windows Vista, much of the material is equally relevant to Windows XP and other versions of the Microsoft Windows operating system.

This book is by the same author as the best-selling and highly acclaimed "Computing for the Older Generation" (BP601).

About the Author

Jim Gatenby trained as a Chartered Mechanical Engineer and initially worked at Rolls-Royce Ltd using computers in the analysis of jet engine performance. He obtained a Master of Philosophy degree in Mathematical Education by research at Loughborough University of Technology and taught mathematics and computing in school for many years before becoming a full-time author. His most recent teaching posts included Head of Computer Studies and Information Technology Coordinator. The author has written many books in the fields of educational computing and Microsoft Windows, including many of the titles in the highly successful Older Generation series from Bernard Babani (publishing) Ltd.

The author has considerable experience of teaching students of all ages and abilities, in school and in adult education. For several years he successfully taught the well-established CLAIT course and also GCSE Computing and Information Technology.

Trademarks

Microsoft, Windows, Windows XP, Windows Vista, Windows 7, Windows Mail, Office 2007, Word and Excel are either trademarks or registered trademarks of Microsoft Corporation. Norton AntiVirus and Norton 360 are trademarks of Symantec Corporation. F-Secure Internet Security is a trademark or registered trademark of F-Secure Corporation. AVG Anti-Virus is a trademark or registered trademark of AVG Technologies. BT is a registered trademark of British Telecommunications plc.

All other brand and product names used in this book are recognized as trademarks or registered trademarks, of their respective companies.

Acknowledgements

I would like to thank my wife Jill and our son David for their help and support during the preparation of this book.

Contents

Conventions Used in this Book

Words which appear on the screen in menus, etc., are shown in the text in bold, for example, **Print Preview**.

Technical terms for devices which may be unfamiliar to the reader are introduced in italics, for example, *wireless router.*

Certain words appear on the screen using the American spelling, such as **Disk Cleanup** for example. Where the text refers directly to an item displayed on the screen, the American spelling is used.

Mouse Operation

Throughout this book, the following terms are used to describe the operation of the mouse:

Click

A single press of the left-hand mouse button.

Double-click

Two presses of the left-hand mouse button, in rapid succession.

Right-click

A single press of the right-hand mouse button.

Drag and Drop

Keep the left-hand or right-hand button held down and move the mouse, before releasing the button to transfer a screen object to a new position.

Further Reading

If you enjoy reading this book and find it helpful, you may be interested in the companion book by the same author, **An Introduction to the Internet for the Older Generation (BP711)** from Bernard Babani (publishing) Ltd and available from all good bookshops.

Computers in the Home

Introduction

Whatever your previous experience, there's never been a better time to get involved in computing, for the following reasons:

- Computers are nowadays much easier to use — you no longer need to be a "geek" or technical expert.

- Computing equipment is cheaper than ever before.

- There is an abundance of good software for every conceivable task.

- The Internet has created a wealth of opportunities for learning, leisure and working from home.

This chapter looks at some of the ways you might use computers in the home and in particular:

- Choosing between a laptop or desktop computer.

- Deciding on suitable location(s) in your home.

- Connecting the cables and starting up.

Not long ago, laptops were inferior to desktop computers in several respects. Recently, however, laptops have improved and are currently outselling desktop machines. If you want to use the computer on the move, in hotels and on the train, for example, then the laptop is the only choice. If your computer will mostly remain in one place in your home or office, then the desktop machine may be a better choice.

> *Computing jargon has been avoided wherever possible in this book; explanations of essential jargon are given at the end of some chapters, where necessary. For more detailed help on computing hardware and understanding jargon please refer to Chapter 9.*

Advantages of the Laptop Computer

- Can be used anywhere in the home and on the move, in hotels or on the train, etc.

- Doesn't need a mains power supply (some of the time).

- Fewer cables and power points are needed.

- Takes up less room in the home — at the end of a session the laptop can be stowed away in a drawer or cupboard.

Shown below on the left is a typical laptop computer; the touch pad and buttons at the centre front replace the mouse used on desktop machines. If you prefer to use a mouse, it's quite easy to plug in a wireless or USB device, as discussed shortly.

A laptop computer with its smaller relation, the netbook

The small laptop shown above on the right is one of a new generation of highly portable computers, known as *netbooks*, this particular example being an Elonex Webbook as described on the next page.

The Netbook Computer

The *netbook* is a very small laptop with a screen size of just 8 to 10 inches so that it can more easily be carried in a bag or briefcase, etc. The netbook bridges the gap between "Internet-enabled" *smartphones* like the Blackberry and the iPhone and the conventional laptop computer.

We recently obtained an Elonex Webbook, an example of a netbook, as shown on the right of the picture on the previous page. After using the Webbook for some time I have been impressed by the overall performance and quality of the machine. The Webbook is "wireless-ready" and was easily connected to the Internet via our wireless router, straight out of the box. The small screen is very clear — much better than our older full-size laptop with a bigger, 15-inch screen. The computer happily runs the Windows XP operating system pre-installed on the machine.

There is no built-in CD/DVD drive but with three USB ports (discussed in Chapter 2, Connecting the Peripherals), it's a simple matter to plug in an external drive. It's also possible to connect a full size keyboard and mouse wirelessly or via the USB ports. A VGA port enables a full-size monitor to be connected.

At around £190-£300, netbook computers provide a highly portable and cost-effective way to get onto the Internet and also carry out the full range of activities such as word processing, spreadsheets, music and e-mail. Some netbooks run the Linux operating system rather than Windows XP and may have a *solid-state drive* for storage instead of the usual hard disc drive.

Expanding a Laptop or Netbook Computer

If you are working on a laptop or netbook at home for long periods, you may want to benefit from a full-size monitor, keyboard and mouse; these components can easily be connected to a laptop computer, as described in Chapter 2, Connecting the Peripherals.

Advantages of the Desktop Computer

- Usually has a better screen than a typical laptop.
- "Proper" full-size QWERTY keyboard and a mouse.
- There is plenty of room inside the desktop machine to add expansion cards and repairs are easily carried out.
- Components for a desktop computer are generally cheaper than those for the laptop machine.
- A desktop computer generally runs cooler than a laptop.
- Desktop machines have a separate keypad for entering numerical data (as do some more expensive laptops).

A desktop computer with colour laser printer

In the above computer system the base or tower unit is located underneath the work surface on a special platform in the purpose-built computer desk.

Homes With More Than One Computer

Computers are now relatively cheap and many homes may have several machines, as in my own home. There is a laptop machine which can be used anywhere in the house. Tucked away in a corner of the lounge we have a family desktop machine used mainly by my wife and myself; our son has a desktop machine in his bedroom. In the garden there is a summerhouse which has been adapted as a home office, with another desktop machine on which books like this one are produced. The machines are connected via a wireless network so they can all share a single broadband Internet connection. Wireless networks are discussed in more detail later.

Using the Laptop

The laptop machine is used mainly by my wife, in any room in the house or out in the garden on a warm day. A disadvantage is that it can only be used for a few hours before the battery needs recharging. Typical uses are browsing the Internet for information on any subject under the sun — online shopping, choosing and booking flights and holidays, solving difficult crossword clues and e-mailing electronic greetings cards containing animations, music and personal messages.

The Family Desktop Machine

In addition to browsing the World Wide Web, it's very useful to be able to print out your own bank statements, transfer money and pay bills. This computer is also used to edit, print and e-mail digital photographs. You can look for a second-hand car on the Auto Trader Web site or sell surplus household items on eBay. The family computer is also used for downloading music and video and recording onto a CD or DVD. Apart from producing letters and reports and managing accounts on a spreadsheet program like Microsoft Excel, the computer is an excellent tool for researching your ancestry, especially since entire census data is available and being added to regularly.

This computer has a multi-function colour inkjet printer or MFP. This cost under £40 and doubles up as a colour photocopier and scanner. There are slots on the front of the printer to allow memory cards from a digital camera to be inserted, enabling photos to be printed directly. A set of ink cartridges for this printer can be obtained for under £10 after shopping around on the Internet.

Multi-function inkjet printer

The Home Office Computer

The computer in my home office is a desktop machine, equipped with a colour laser printer; the colour printer is needed for checking the draft pages in books like this one.

Colour laser printers can be obtained for under £200. If your work doesn't require colour then monochrome laser printers are available for under £100. If

Colour laser printer

you do a lot of printing, the extra speed of a laser printer will be beneficial. Toner for a laser printer may cost £50-£80. A multi-function laser printer can also be used as a photocopier and scanner.

If you only have one family computer, there can be problems; what happens if two people want to use the computer at the same time? Additionally, if your family computer is also used for work or business, it's probably not ideal to clutter your lounge with paperwork and other office paraphernalia.

The Home Office

If you're using a computer for serious purposes such as working from home, writing a novel or parish magazine or running a small business, it's better if you can set up a separate dedicated home office. If you're fortunate enough to have a spare room, this may be ideal. It will be warm and secure and will probably already have the necessary power points. There's no need these days for such a room to have a cabled telephone extension; provided you have a telephone socket somewhere in your home, an inexpensive *wireless router* will ensure that your home office computer can connect to the Internet from anywhere in your house or garden.

If you don't have a spare room but still want to set up a separate home office, perhaps you have a garden with space for a suitable shed. Purpose-built home offices can be expensive but my solution was to buy a wooden summerhouse; with the addition of insulation, soundproofing and double glazing this has made a very warm, quiet office with very few distractions.

The Shed — a summerhouse used as a home office

If your home office is a shed in the garden, you really need to have a permanent power cable installed, rather than rely on temporary extension leads. This power supply should use special *armoured cable*, preferably buried at least two feet underground. The armoured cable has a metal sheath to prevent it being severed with a spade next time you, or those who come after you, are digging the garden. Even if you install the power cable yourself, it's a legal requirement to have it checked and certified as safe by a qualified electrician.

In my experience, you can't have too much desk space; perfectly good office furniture can be bought cheaply from second-hand retailers. A purpose-built computer desk with special holes for the cables and a lower platform for the base unit is a good investment for the home office. A wireless keyboard and mouse help to de-clutter the desk; the wireless mouse moves more easily than the cabled variety.

Inside the Shed — a wireless mouse and keyboard and floor-mounted tower unit ensure plenty of desk space

Working from Home

If you are retired or approaching retirement, working at home can be a rewarding and interesting way to keep yourself active; perhaps you could continue in your previous employment, possibly working fewer hours or in a consultancy capacity. Or perhaps you could write up a history of your parish or village and get it printed and published. Some people start a Web site for like-minded individuals to share helpful information.

Having taken early retirement from teaching in my fifties I was fortunate to be able to start a new career as an author working from home; thanks mainly to Michael Babani at Bernard Babani (publishing) Ltd, I have now had nearly 30 books published. If you've worked in a trade or profession for a good many years, perhaps there's a book in you that will allow you to pass on your experience to the younger generation. Maybe, like the vet James Herriot or the school inspector Gervase Phinn, you've amassed lots of amusing anecdotes which can be turned into a best seller.

One advantage of the separate home office in the garden is that it's a bit like going out to work, even if it's only a few yards down the garden. There's also the added bonus of not having to spend stressful hours commuting to and from work. You are away from the distractions and interruptions of your home and, if you have a partner, they get the house to themselves for a few hours. When you finish work you close the office door and leave your work behind. Working from home has the advantage that you can choose your own hours and, with fewer distractions, can be more productive. On the negative side, toiling for hours in a home office is a solitary activity, especially for someone used to working with other people.

Installing a Home Computer

The laptop computer doesn't need much installing since it's self-contained and only needs a single power point. However, the laptop will need to be connected to the Internet and this is discussed in Chapter 3, Getting Online.

The desktop computer will need a minimum of four power points but preferably six, to power the base unit, monitor, printer and possible additions such as a scanner, speakers and a desk light. Some extension leads have a built-in surge protector which guards against sudden "spikes" or variations in power; otherwise you can buy a separate plug-in surge protector costing about £5, which is inserted between your mains power point and the extension lead. If you live in an area where power cuts are common, a UPS (Uninterruptable Power Supply) will keep your computer powered up for long enough to shut it down correctly. (If a computer is not shut down correctly, e.g. by a sudden failure of the power supply, you are likely to lose your current work and there may be damage to other files on the computer).

The main part of the desktop computer is the *base unit*, also called the *tower unit*. This is the "engine room" of the computer and is a metal or plastic box containing all of the components discussed in Chapter 9, such as the memory, processor, motherboard and hard disc drive. The base unit may be placed on the desk alongside of the monitor although I prefer to put the base unit on the floor to save desk space. The essential items to connect are the monitor, keyboard and mouse; in addition there may be a printer and speakers. It's also necessary to connect the power cable between a power socket and the power supply unit in the back of the computer. It's best to leave the connection of the power cable until everything else has been connected.

The Monitor

The latest flat screen TFT (Thin Film Transistor) monitors give an excellent display and take up very little desk space compared with the earlier Cathode Ray Tube monitors. Some TFT monitors also contain built-in speakers. A very good 19-inch TFT monitor can be bought for under £100 with a 22-inch model costing nearer £200. Larger monitors are available but are much more expensive. (Monitors are measured diagonally across the screen.) Some monitors plug into a power point using their own cable and plug, while others have a female connection on their power cable which plugs into the power supply unit at the back of the computer. A video cable connects the monitor to the computer via a 15-pin D-type connector, shown right.

The Keyboard and Mouse

The standard way to attach the keyboard and mouse to the computer is via special cables known as *PS/2 connectors*. The cables are permanently attached to the keyboard and mouse and fit into PS/2 sockets or ports on the back of the computer. The keyboard port is normally purple while the mouse port is green. Care is needed to ensure the pins are lined up properly.

You should now be able to connect the main power cable and switch on. There will be a switch on the front of the base unit and

another on the power supply unit at the back, normally near the top, shown above to the right of **230V**. The monitor will have its own power switch on the front. The computer should now start up and after a short time display the Windows Desktop. If there is no screen display, check that all units are powered up, (indicated by green lights) and that the video cable to the monitor is firmly connected.

Shutting Down

To prevent loss of files, always save your work and shut down using the correct procedure. This means clicking (surprisingly) the **Start** button and then allowing the cursor to hover over the small arrow to the right of the padlock shown on the right. Then click **Shut Down** from the menu which appears, as shown below.

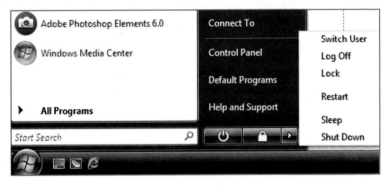

Hybrid Desktop Computers

Desktop computers are rather like the woodman's axe which had had five new handles and three new heads. Similarly you don't need to buy a complete new computer system every time you want to upgrade. You can always add a better keyboard, mouse or monitor to an existing base unit. Or you can buy a new base unit and keep your existing peripheral devices. In fact you can mix and match these components in any way you like. As mentioned in Chapter 9, the performance of a computer can often be improved by modifying the base unit itself with improved internal components; these include extra memory, a faster processor, and better graphics card.

2

Connecting the Peripherals

Introduction

The peripheral devices include the mouse and keyboard, printer, modem/router, flash drive, (also known as a *memory key* or *memory stick*) and speakers and headphones, etc. These devices all plug into sockets or *ports* on the case of the computer. The ports connect to the computer's motherboard. In the case of a laptop the ports are on the sides of the machine; on the desktop computer the ports are mainly on the back.

Types of Port

Most computers are fitted with several different types of port, although, as discussed shortly, the USB port is taking over as the preferred connection for many types of peripheral device.

PS/2 Ports

The green PS/2 port shown on the right is used to connect the mouse cable while the purple PS/2 port is used for the keyboard connection. USB mice and keyboards are also available; these have cables which connect to any of the USB ports on the base unit, as shown on the next page. Another option is to use a *wireless* keyboard and mouse. These are battery powered and get their signal from a small wireless "dongle" plugged into one of the USB ports.

The Serial Port

At one time these were the standard connection for mice and modems. There were often two serial ports, also known as *RS232 ports* and *communication ports*, usually referred to as COM1 and COM2. Shown on the right is a 9-pin male serial port.

13

The Parallel Port

Until the arrival of USB ports, this was the standard method of connecting printers and scanners. It's also known as the printer port and Centronics port (after a manufacturer of printers). Data is transmitted in a parallel stream of bits, unlike the serial port, in which data is transmitted one bit at a time. Shown on the right is a 25-pin female parallel port.

The Ethernet Port

Although many homes now use wireless networks, many businesses prefer *cabled* networks. These are acknowledged to be faster than wireless networks but do require holes to be drilled in walls and cabling installed throughout the building. Most wired networks use *Ethernet* technology; this refers to the cables, built-in network adaptors and Ethernet ports, as shown on the right. An Ethernet port and network adaptor are fitted as standard to most computers.

Even on a wireless network it's often recommended that the initial setting up is done using an Ethernet cable between the router and the computer.

The Graphics VGA Port

This is the standard connection for monitors used on home and small business computers. Shown on the right is a 15-pin VGA port which accepts a standard monitor cable. These are present on laptops as well as desktop computers, allowing a separate, full size monitor to be connected to a laptop.

The Audio or Sound Ports

The audio ports shown on the right connect audio devices to the sound facilities on the motherboard or on a separate internal sound expansion card. The green port is used for sound output to speakers or headphones, pink is for input from a microphone while light blue is used for audio input, such as from an external CD drive.

USB (Universal Serial Bus) Ports

These are a relatively new type of socket and have transformed the way peripheral devices are connected. The USB ports are small rectangular slots; on a desktop computer there are  usually four USB ports at the back of the base unit and sometimes a further two at the front. Laptops usually have three or four USB ports on the side of the computer.

The USB ports can be used to connect virtually any type of peripheral device, such as:

Mouse	Keyboard
Inkjet or Laser Printer	Flash drive
Scanner	External hard disc drive
Digital camera	Wireless adaptor
Modem	Headphones

The USB port has many advantages over the earlier serial and parallel ports, which were bulky and expensive:

- USB devices such as a digital camera, for example, can be plugged in or removed while the computer is up and running. There's no need to shut down first. This is known as "hot swapping".

- USB devices transfer data much faster than earlier technology.

- USB connections are simple and light and easy to plug in and remove.

- Some USB devices work as soon as they are plugged in, without the need for any special installation software, known as *device drivers*.

- The current specification in general use is USB 2.0, which is approximately ten times faster than the earlier USB 1.1, still in use on some computers. USB 2.0 is also known as Hi-Speed USB.

- If your computer only has USB 1.1 ports and you buy a USB 2.0 device, such as a flash drive, the device will still work. However you will not benefit from the extra performance of the USB 2.0 device. Similarly if a USB 2.0 device uses a connecting cable, the cable must be of the USB 2.0 standard to obtain the full performance.

- An even faster specification, called USB 3.0 or USB SuperSpeed has been developed but USB 3.0 devices are not widely available at the time of writing.

Checking Your Computer for USB 2.0 Capability

If you have a new computer it will almost certainly be equipped for USB 2.0 devices; older machines may only provide the earlier and slower USB 1.1 standard. To benefit from USB 2.0, your machine must have an **Enhanced Host Controller**, as shown below; this is displayed after clicking **Start**, **Control Panel** and double-clicking the **Device Manager** icon, shown on the right. Double-click **Universal Serial Bus controllers** shown highlighted in blue below to display the full list of USB devices. The word **Enhanced** below indicates that this particular computer can support USB 2.0 devices.

Device Manager

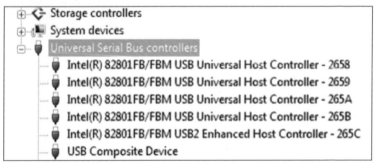

Adding Extra USB Ports

It's theoretically possible to connect 127 USB devices to a single computer, although it's hard to imagine how this might be necessary for a home computer user. However, if your computer only has 2, 3 or 4 USB ports, you may sometimes need some more. In the case of a desktop machine, there are often four USB ports on the back and two on the front. If you need to keep "hot swapping" USB devices such as USB flash drives, digital camera or headphones for example, this may be inconvenient if the ports on the back of the machine are not very accessible. You may also need to have several other USB devices permanently connected such as a printer, modem or router, wireless network adaptor "dongle" and possibly a USB keyboard and mouse.

If you are short of USB ports, a simple solution is to buy a *USB hub* typically containing 4 or 7 ports. The 4-port hub usually takes its power from the computer, whereas the larger hubs have a separate power supply cable.

A 4-port USB hub

Alternatively, you can obtain a 4-port *USB 2.0 Expansion card* which plugs into one of the PCI slots on the motherboard of a desktop computer, as discussed in Chapter 9. This provides four extra USB 2.0 ports on the back of the computer.

A 4-port USB 2.0 expansion card

Laptop users can plug a USB 2.0 4-port *PCMCIA Expansion card* into the PCMCIA slot on the side of their machine. All of these devices can typically be bought for around £10 or less.

Installing USB Devices

USB devices are very easy to plug into the small rectangular USB ports on the computer; they only fit one way round and no force is required. Some devices, such as printers, also require their own separate power supply. Other devices, such as plug-in flash drive "dongles", take their power off the computer itself.

When you plug a USB keyboard or mouse into a computer it should work straightaway. This is also true for some USB flash drives, USB external hard disc drives and wireless adaptors.

Other devices, such as USB printers, require software called *device drivers* to enable the printer to work with a particular version of Windows, such as Windows XP or Windows Vista.

When you connect a new USB device to a computer, it is detected straightaway. Windows contains some device drivers within its own resources and attempts to find a driver for the new device. If a suitable driver is found, all being well the new device will be installed and ready for use very quickly. If a suitable driver is not found, Windows requests that you insert the software CD which came with your device. Then the device is installed.

If you don't have the driver software for your particular USB device, such as a printer, it's usually possible to download one from the Web site of the manufacturer of the device. When Windows Vista first appeared, some existing printers, for example, would not work with Vista. New Vista drivers had to be downloaded from the Internet to make the devices work .

If you allow Windows to detect a new device and then select a Windows driver, it's possible that the device may not work properly. This might occur if Windows has selected an unsuitable driver. For this reason, some manufacturers of devices such as printers recommend that you install their software drivers first, before connecting and switching on the device. This ensures that after detecting a new device, Windows uses the driver supplied by the device manufacturer, not a driver selected by Windows.

Installing a USB Printer

Before installing a new printer, always read the manufacturer's instructions. They may tell you to install the driver software from the CD <u>before</u> connecting the USB cable to the computer and switching the printer on. Then during the installation you are instructed to connect the cables and switch the printer on.

The next few pages describe the setting up of a Canon laser printer; with this particular printer you are instructed to connect the printer to the USB port on the computer and switch on, <u>before</u> installing the driver software. On a USB cable, the connector at the device end is different from the connector at the computer end, so the cable cannot be incorrectly fitted.

When the printer is connected and switched on, it is quickly detected, as shown by the **Found New Hardware** window on the right. Then the **Found**  **New Hardware Wizard** opens and asks for your permission for Windows to connect to the **Windows Update Web** site to search for a suitable driver. However, this should not be necessary, as a CD containing the driver software is normally supplied along with a new device such as a printer. So you can simply select **No, not this time** and then click **Next**. The **Found New Hardware Wizard** then asks you to insert the CD which came with your hardware, as shown below.

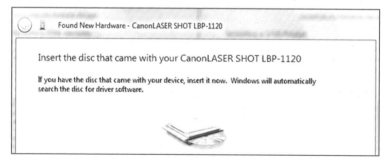

Once the CD is detected, the wizard asks you to choose the best driver for your hardware from a drop-down list, as shown below. The list includes drivers for the various versions of Windows such as Windows XP and Windows Vista.

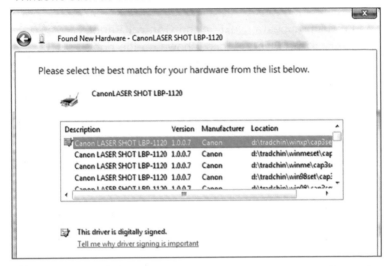

After clicking **Next** you are asked to wait while the software is installed before the following window appears and you click **Finish** to complete the operation. If you wish you can also print a test page.

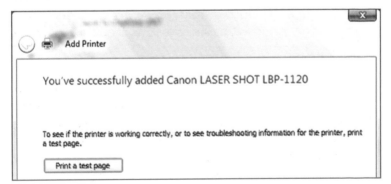

Checking the New Printer

The **Control Panel** in Windows XP and Vista allows you to alter various settings for all of your devices, including your printer.

Click the **Start** button at the bottom left of the screen and then click **Control Panel** from the Start Menu which appears. Next, in the **Control Panel**, double-click the **Printers** icon, shown on the right. The **Printers** window opens, displaying icons for all of the printer drivers installed on your computer.

Printers

In the extract above, the tick next to the **Canon** indicates that it is the *default printer*, i.e. the printer automatically selected in any printing operation, for example, when printing a letter.

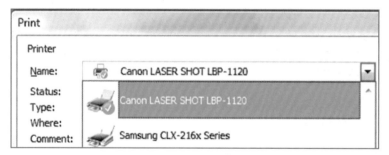

To select a different printer in Word or Excel, etc., click the small downward pointing arrow shown on the right above, in the **Print** dialogue box. Then click an alternative printer from the drop-down list, such as the **Samsung** printer in this example. Obviously to print from the selected printer it must be switched on and connected to your computer with a USB cable .

Changing the Default Printer

In the **Printers** window shown on the previous page, the **Samsung** can be set as the default printer after right-clicking over its icon. Then select **Set as Default Printer** from the menu. **Printing Preferences** on the right allows you to change many of the printer settings such as paper size and portrait or landscape orientation.

Open

Run as administrator ▶

Set as Default Printer

Printing Preferences...

Pause Printing

Cancel All Documents

Sharing...

Use Printer Online

If you double-click the icon for the default printer, the window shown below appears.

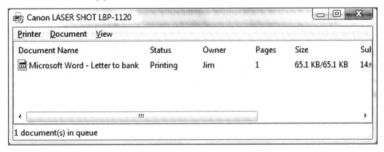

Canon LASER SHOT LBP-1120					
Printer Document View					
Document Name	Status	Owner	Pages	Size	Sul
Microsoft Word - Letter to bank	Printing	Jim	1	65.1 KB/65.1 KB	14:⊡
1 document(s) in queue					

This shows the status of any current print jobs; clicking **Printer** shown on the left of the menu bar above displays a list of options to pause or cancel a print job. This can be useful if something goes wrong with the current printing operation, for example if you have incorrectly set the orientation of the paper. The menu under **Printer** shown above has a **Sharing....** option. This also appears on the menu at the top of this page. Clicking this option leads to the **Properties** dialogue box allowing you to switch on **Share this printer,** allowing several computers to share one printer on a network.

Using a Netbook or Laptop as a Desktop

It's a simple matter to attach a bigger monitor or full-size keyboard and mouse to a laptop. (On this page the term laptop also refers to the smaller netbook machines). This might be helpful, for example, if you are doing a lot of word processing or data entry and your eyesight is not as good as it used to be. A good 19 inch TFT monitor can be bought for under £100 and this simply connects to the 15-pin D-type VGA connector on the laptop. A full-size USB keyboard and mouse can be added for about £15 or less. These plug into the USB ports on the laptop and are immediately detected and ready for use. Once the mouse, keyboard and monitor are connected, a couple of function key presses may be needed on the laptop to bring up the laptop screen display on the separate monitor. The laptop or netbook can now be used with all the ergonomic advantages of the bigger desktop machine, as shown below.

A netbook computer connected to a full-size monitor, keyboard and mouse

Jargon at a Glance

Control Panel A feature in Windows XP and Vista which enables settings to be altered and hardware and software to be removed.

Device driver Software which enables a device to work with a particular version of Windows, such as Windows XP or Vista. A new device package normally includes a CD containing the driver software; Windows itself also contains drivers for many devices.

Enhanced Host Controller Hardware on the motherboard which is needed to support USB 2.0 devices

Hot swapping Connecting or disconnecting a USB device while the computer is up and running.

Parallel port (also known as a **Centronics port**) Connection socket for earlier types of printers, etc., now superseded by USB devices.

Printers A window accessed from the Control Panel, allowing the printer settings to be altered.

Serial port A connection socket for earlier types of mouse and modem, etc. Also known as communication ports, COM1 or COM2.

USB (Universal Serial Bus) A technology for connecting peripheral devices to a computer through simple sockets or ports on the computer. USB provides much faster data transfer than earlier connection methods, such as serial or parallel ports.

USB 2.0 Also known as USB High-Speed. Currently the most widely used USB standard, much faster than the earlier USB 1.1.

USB 3.0 or USB SuperSpeed An even faster new USB design; USB 3.0 devices are not yet widely available at the time of writing.

USB expansion card A small circuit board containing several extra USB ports. Desktop machines use a PCI expansion card fitted internally to the computer's motherboard; laptops use a PCMCIA card which plugs into a slot in the side of the computer.

USB Hub A device which plugs into a USB port and provides several extra USB ports.

3

Getting Online

Introduction

In the last few years the Internet has become an essential part of the lives of many people and some of us probably wonder how we ever managed without it. Listed below are just a few examples of the way the Internet is used in our household:

- Ordering the weekly supermarket shopping to be delivered to our door; the total time for the entire "shop" is usually only about 10-15 minutes .

- Communicating with friends and relatives by e-mail, including photographs and electronic greetings cards.

- Checking out holiday destinations, booking flights and accommodation, checking in online for certain flights.

- Planning journeys using online maps and route planners and Google Earth to look at particular areas.

- Checking and printing bank statements, setting up standing orders and making electronic fund transfers.

- Comparing saving and investment offers.

- Buying books and other items from Amazon and other online stores, usually delivered within one or two days.

- Selling unwanted household items on eBay.

- Downloading music and software, obtaining latest *device drivers* to make computing equipment work.

- Using the RSPB Web site to identify birds from pictures, bird songs and video clips.

- Finding information on any subject using Web sites such as Google, Wikipedia and HowStuffWorks.

Broadband

For several years the only way home users were able to connect to the Internet was using a device called a *dial-up* modem; this linked the computer to an ordinary telephone line. In recent years a much faster system known as *broadband* has become the standard; this enables you to surf the Internet more quickly and download large files such as videos and music — painfully laborious tasks on the older and slower dial-up systems.

Most broadband services still use the BT telephone lines, but modifications must be made to your local telephone exchange before you can receive broadband. In addition the line to your home has to be *activated* by BT. You also need a special *ADSL modem* or a *router* to connect to a broadband Internet service.

Some remote areas of Britain still cannot receive broadband because their telephone exchanges have not been modified. If you already have access to an Internet computer, you can find out which broadband services are available in your area by logging on to **www.broadbandchecker.co.uk** and entering your postcode. An example of the results is shown below:

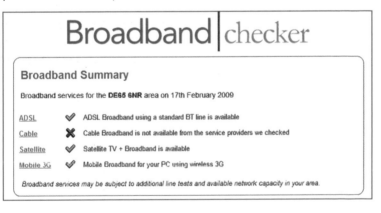

If you don't already have access to an Internet computer, you should be able to log on in a local library or Internet cafe.

Many people use the ADSL Broadband service provided by BT; some companies, such as AOL and Tiscali, deliver an Internet service over the BT phone lines. Virgin Media provide Cable Broadband to areas covered by cable television and Sky offer TV and Broadband via satellite. Some mobile phone companies provide an Internet connection using a modem which plugs into a USB port on your computer. In some remote areas where ADSL lines are not available, a *wireless* broadband service is provided.

Internet Service Providers

There is a bewildering number of Internet Service Providers but, if you already have access to the Internet, you can look at several Web sites comparing the various offers from the ISPs. These comparisons cover such details as the monthly cost (anything from £7 to £25) and the maximum download speed (currently 8Mbps is common). (Please see Chapter 9 for an explanation of Mbps or megabits per second). Most Internet service providers will tie you into a minimum contract time, typically 12 or 18 months. Some Internet Service Providers include a free router valued at about £50 and may also provide the cables and filters and software to complete your setup. Shown below is an extract from the Broadband-Finder Web site (**www.broadband-finder.co.uk**). This site also includes an option to enter your postcode and find all the services available in your area.

Provider	Package	Usage	Speed	Download Limit	Setup Cost	Contract Period	Monthly Cost	1st Year Cost **
BT	**Online Exclusive:** BT Broadband - Option 1 FREE new Wireless Black BT Home Hub available with £20 off your bill with Option 1. Option 1 now comes with 8Mbps download speed and a 10GB monthly download limit. Order online now or call free on 0800 328 1522. More >	LIGHT	Up To 8Mbps	10GB	FREE	18 Months	£7.78	£164.1
	Recommended: TalkTalk Broadband - Essentials Create your personalised broadband package with TalkTalk 'Essentials', the new broadband package from TalkTalk. Also includes a FREE wireless router. Order online or call 0800 049 7842 to order over the	MEDIUM	Up To 8Mbps	40GB	£29.99	18 Months	£6.49	£107.8

Broadband Requirements

The next few pages explain how to set up a computer to use an ADSL broadband service based on the BT telephone lines. The essential requirements are:

- An account with an Internet Service Provider such as BT, AOL or Tiscali, etc.

- A BT telephone socket and a telephone line which has been tested by BT and activated for ADSL broadband.

- An ADSL modem or a *router* containing an ADSL modem. Many Internet Service Providers now include a free router as part of the package.

- One or more *filters* allowing a telephone socket to be used for broadband and phone calls at the same time .

- A cable to connect the modem or router to the filter.

- When a router is used, an Ethernet cable to connect a computer, at least during the initial setting up.

- A *network adaptor* in each desktop machine connected to the Internet. This may be in the form of a PCI expansion card fitted inside of the computer; alternatively the adaptor can be a "dongle" which plugs into a USB port on the computer. Laptop computers normally have built-in wireless networking capability.

- Software and instructions for setting up the modem or router, usually on a CD included in the startup package from the Internet Service Provider, such as BT.

- In the case of a wireless router, a *network name* and a *security key* to prevent other people from logging on to your Internet connection from outside of your home. (Wireless home networks may have a range of 100-300 feet, depending on obstructions like walls and floors.)

The Wireless Router

A wireless router with a built-in ADSL modem is one of the most popular ways of connecting to the Internet. Many Internet Service Providers include a free router in their startup kit. A wireless router will be fine even if you only have one computer; if you have more than one computer, the wireless router will allow them all to be connected to the Internet simultaneously using a single telephone socket.

The wireless network is a good solution for most home users since it avoids the alternative system of drilling holes in walls, etc., and trailing Ethernet cables all round the house or flat. I have found wireless technology to be extremely reliable using computers scattered about the house in different rooms, requiring the wireless signals to pass through several walls.

The initial setting up of the router may require a computer to be sitting next to the router and connected to it by an Ethernet networking cable. However, once the network is up and running the wireless router can sit on its own next to your telephone socket, with no computers physically connected to it by Ethernet cables. In the example below, our router is placed in the dining room next to the telephone socket, while the computers themselves are in different rooms around the house.

A BT Home Hub router sits almost unobtrusively in the dining room

The Wireless Router Startup Kit

If you subscribe to an Internet Service Provider such as BT, you may obtain a free wireless router and the various components needed to get you started, as shown below.

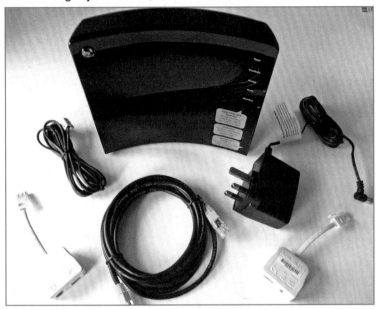

The BT Home Hub wireless router and accessories

In the above photograph, the router itself is the large black box at the rear. On the right is the power supply cable and transformer. The white cables and sockets are known as *filters* or *microfilters*; these plug into the main telephone socket(s) in your home. Each filter itself has two sockets; one socket connects an ordinary telephone handset while the other connects the broadband cable from the router. This is the black cable shown to the left of the router above. The filter enables an ordinary telephone to be used at the same time as the broadband Internet.

The black cable with yellow ends shown above is an Ethernet cable, which may be needed in the initial setting up of the router.

The Router Ports in Detail

Shown below are ports on the rear of the wireless router supplied by BT as part of their broadband package.

The ports on the back of the BT Home Hub wireless router

The left-hand socket in the group above is used for the cable which connects the router to the broadband telephone socket, via a filter, as mentioned on the previous page. The green socket is for a special BT Internet telephone. The four yellow Ethernet sockets have several uses, such as the initial setting up of the router using an Ethernet cable connected to a computer. The Ethernet sockets can also be used to create a *wired network,* using Ethernet cables and adaptors instead of wireless technology. Wired networks are often preferred in business, since they can be faster than wireless and unsightly cables may not be such an issue as they are in a home environment.

On the right of the router above is the socket for the power cable; finally there is a USB socket to connect a USB cable to a USB port on a computer (as an alternative to an Ethernet cable.)

BT Vision

One of the Ethernet sockets on the router can be used to connect an Ethernet cable from the router to a BT Vision digital television box. This allows a large number of Freeview programs to be viewed and recorded; live television can be paused and restarted. A daily program guide can be downloaded and extra programs and films are available on demand, (for a fee).

Instruction Manuals

The router package should also include an instruction manual and a quick-start leaflet; increasingly a more comprehensive instruction manual is provided on the CD which accompanies the router.

Wireless Network Adaptors

Each computer on a wireless network must be equipped with electronic components to enable the computer to detect and communicate with the wireless router. Modern laptop computers are normally supplied with wireless networking capability already built in, although this may need to be switched on.

USB Wireless Network Adaptors

Desktop computers may need to be fitted with a separate *wireless network adaptor*. This may take the form of a "dongle" which plugs into a USB port on the computer. A cable allows the USB network adaptor to be moved about to obtain the best wireless signal.

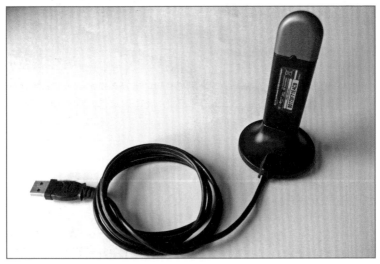

A USB wireless network adaptor

PCI Wireless Network Adaptors

The PCI wireless network adaptor fits inside the cover of the base unit of a desktop computer; it's a simple job to unscrew the cover of the base unit and press the adaptor into a vacant PCI slot on the computer's motherboard, as discussed in Chapter 9.

A wireless network adaptor in the form of a PCI expansion card

A network adaptor may be included in a wireless router package. Otherwise they can be purchased for under £10 from computer shops and by mail order. The package should also include installation instructions and a CD containing the driver software.

802.11 Wireless Protocols

Wireless (or Wi-Fi) equipment such as routers and network adaptors must conform to various *protocols* or technical specifications. Currently most wi-fi equipment is specified as **802.11b**, **802.11g** or the latest protocol, **802.11n**. Check with the router manual to find the **802.11** adaptor specification compatible with your router.

Installing a Wireless Network

Before you can start to set up a wireless network based on a wireless router, your telephone line must be tested and activated for ADSL broadband by BT. If you are using an Internet Service Provider other than BT, they may make the arrangements for you. You might have to wait a week or 10 days for the activation to be effective.

Once the telephone line is activated you can start installing the router. Ideally the router should be in a central position in your home if you are connecting several computers. If possible, avoiding installing the router near to a microwave oven or cordless phones as these may interfere with the broadband.

Place a filter in the main telephone socket in your home. If you want to use an ordinary telephone here, there is a socket for this on the filter. Now connect the special broadband cable (known as an RJ11 cable) from the router to the other socket in the filter. (The broadband and ordinary telephone sockets in the filter are quite different, so you can't connect the cables incorrectly.)

Now connect the power cable from a power point to the router and switch on. Initially the diagnostic lights on the front of the router will flash yellow and then after a minute or two the power, broadband and wireless lights should be constant blue.

Set up a computer within a few feet of the router. This computer should be fitted with a wireless network adaptor as discussed earlier. Most modern laptops have built-in wireless networking capability although this may need to be switched on. Some desktop computers are also "wireless ready" but otherwise they need a USB or PCI wireless adaptor fitted, as discussed earlier. BT provide an installation CD which is intended to be used on every computer, although this is not essential to make the connection to the Internet.

Start up the computer and the small Internet icon (consisting of two monitors) will probably display a red cross; hover the cursor over this icon and it should display the message **Wireless networks**

available, as shown above. Double-click the Internet icon and from the small window which pops up, click **Connect to a network**. A list of nearby wireless networks is displayed, including yours, as shown below:

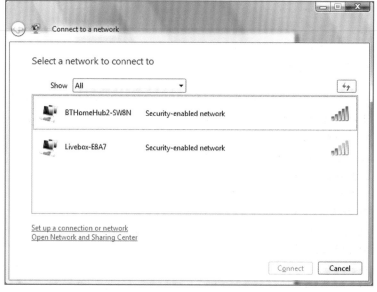

In the above example, two networks have been detected; the name of a network such as **BTHomeHub2-SW8N** is also referred to as the *SSID* or *Service Set Identifier*. Now click the name of your router, such as the **BTHomeHub** and then click the **Connect** button. You must then enter a *wireless key* to make the network secure. The BT security key is displayed on the back of the router and on a small card provided in the router package.

Entering the Security Key

The security key or password must be entered into every computer the first time it is connected to the router. If you don't have a secure network, any of your neighbours or someone nearby with a laptop could use your internet connection and possibly hack into your data.

The dialogue box for entering the security key is shown below.

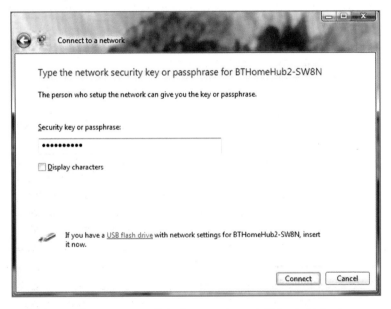

All being well, once you click **Connect** you will be told that you are successfully connected to the router and the Internet. This is also indicated by the Internet icon which should now show two blue monitors with a small image of the globe. If you lose the Internet connection, the globe disappears.

You are now ready to start up your Web browser such as Internet Explorer and start surfing. The above procedure must be repeated for every computer that you want to connect.

Using an Ethernet Cable to Connect a Router

An Ethernet cable, also known as an RJ45 cable, usually with yellow connectors at each end, should be supplied with your router kit. If you are unable, for any reason, to make a wireless connection to the Internet, the Ethernet cable provides a temporary direct link between your router and the computer.

Some routers, such as those made by Belkin and Linksys, require you to connect the computer with an Ethernet cable; then, using a Web browser such as Internet Explorer, type the *IP address* of the router, such as **192.168.2.1** for example, into the browser's address bar, as shown below.

This IP address will connect you to the router in the same way that an IP address can be used to connect to a Web page. You can now set up the router using settings provided by your Internet Service Provider. These might include a username and password and other details such as the type of wireless security, usually either WEP or WPA. These are methods of *encryption* which involves encoding information so that only people with a key can *decipher* it. Please see your router's instruction manual for the precise details for creating a secure network.

Once the router and each computer are set up, it should be possible to dispense with the Ethernet cables and connect to the Internet wirelessly.

With the BT Home Hub router discussed earlier it should not be necessary to connect the computer to the router using an Ethernet cable. This is because the BT Home Hub is already set up and often only requires the wireless key to be entered to make the connection. However, should there be any problems in connecting wirelessly, it might be helpful to plug in the Ethernet cable, connect to the Internet and login to your Internet Service Provider's Web site or router manufacturer to obtain online help.

Checking Your Internet Connection

Right-click the Internet icon at the bottom right of the screen, then click **Network and Sharing Center**. This dialogue box allows you to view many aspects of your new wireless network. You can also set up your network so that files, printers and other resources can be shared by all of the computers on the network.

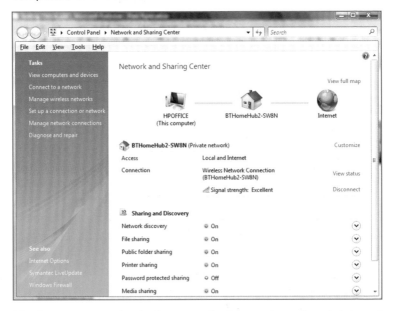

Finally you can check the speed of your broadband Internet connection. At the time of writing, many services offer a download speed of up to 8Mbps. In practice this speed may not be achieved due to technical limitations such as your distance from the local telephone exchange. You can check your broadband speed by logging onto a Web site such as:

www.broadbandspeedchecker.co.uk

Now follow the instructions on the screen to test the upload and download speeds of your broadband connection.

Summary: Getting Online

The following list outlines the general method of connecting to the Internet using a BT ADSL broadband telephone line and a wireless router:

1. Check that you can receive ADSL broadband from your local telephone exchange.

2. Sign up with an Internet Service Provider.

3. Wait for BT to test and activate your telephone line to receive broadband.

4. Obtain a wireless router with a built-in ADSL modem. Your Internet Service Provider may supply this.

5. Insert a microfilter into the main telephone socket in your home.

6. Insert the cable from a telephone handset into the telephone socket in the microfilter.

7. Connect the broadband cable from the router into the broadband socket in the microfilter.

8. Connect the power lead for the router and switch on. The power light on the router should be on; then the wireless and broadband lights should stop flashing.

9. Set up a "wireless enabled" computer near to the router. If necessary attach an RJ45 Ethernet cable between the router and the computer.

10. Start up the computer and connect to the Internet using a Web browser such as Internet Explorer. Enter the wireless key and/or any other information for your router or supplied by your Internet Service Provider.

11. Remove the Ethernet cable and repeat steps 9 and 10 for any other computers on the network.

12. You should now be able to connect wirelessly to the Internet from any computer on the network.

Jargon at a Glance

Activation BT test and prepare your broadband Internet telephone line so that it's ready for use on the *activation date*.

ADSL (Asymmetric Digital Subscriber Line) Technology which transmits broadband data over copper telephone lines.

Broadband Very fast transfer of data and information over the Internet via ADSL telephone lines, cable, satellite and wireless, etc.

Encryption A method of "scrambling" wireless data so that it can't easily be decoded by a "hacker". WEP is an earlier form of coding while WPA is a later, more secure system.

Ethernet Cables, adaptors and ports used to connect devices using wires known as RJ45 cables.

Filter or microfilter A connector allowing broadband and an ordinary telephone to share a telephone socket simultaneously.

Google Internet "search engine" allowing you to type in keywords to find information on any subject, also images, maps and news.

IP Address (Internet Protocol) A numeric string, e.g. **198.168.2.1** which uniquely identifies a computer or device on the Internet, similar to a Web address such as **www.babanibooks.com**.

ISP (Internet Service Provider) Company charging users a subscription to connect to the Internet via their *server* computers.

Modem Device for converting computer data for transmission over telephone lines. Broadband usually requires an ADSL modem or a *router* with a built-in ADSL modem.

Network adaptor A device connecting a computer to a local area network. May be an internal PCI card or external USB "dongle".

Router Device allowing several computers to share a single Internet connection and share files and printers, wirelessly or with cables.

Wireless (Wi-Fi) protocol Technical specification used to define standards of wireless equipment, such as **802.11b**, **g**, or **n**.

Wireless key Password used to prevent unauthorised access to a wireless router.

Exploring the Internet and E-mail

Introduction

The Internet is a worldwide network of millions of computers known as *servers*; these computers store billions of pages of information, making up the World Wide Web. Internet Explorer is known as a *Web browser*, a program designed to help you find and display Web pages on a particular subject. Internet Explorer connects to the servers holding the information you require, anywhere in the world. Then the information is *downloaded* to your computer, which is known as a *network client* as opposed to a *network server*.

Internet Explorer can be launched by clicking the **Start** button at the bottom left of the Windows desktop and then selecting **Internet Explorer** from the top of the Start Menu.

Your Home Page

Clicking **Internet Explorer** above connects to the Internet and opens at the Web page which has been set up as your Home Page. There may be a key on your keyboard, usually marked with an icon for a house, taking you straight to your Home Page with a single press. You can change your Home Page in Internet Explorer after selecting **Tools** and **Internet Options**.

Searching for Information

The MSN UK Home Page has a Search Bar into which you type keywords which precisely identify the subject you are interested in, such as "**the red squirrel**", for example, as shown below.

When you click the magnifying glass icon shown on the right above, a list of Web sites appears as shown below; these contain your keywords somewhere within their pages.

Click on the underlined blue links above to have a look at the actual Web pages. The sites near the top of the list are usually the most relevant to your search.

Please note in the above list of search results there is one result which pops up near the top of many searches; this is **Wikipedia**, a free, online encyclopaedia, partly compiled by volunteers.

You can concentrate your search on various categories such as **News**, **Maps** and **Images**, etc., by clicking the category name as shown in the MSN Search Bar at the top of this page.

Google

A search engine is a computer program designed to find information from the Internet. Although you will probably find searching using the Search Bar in MSN perfectly satisfactory, Google has established itself as the leading program in this field. Google is free and can be obtained after entering **www.google.co.uk** into the Address Bar at the top of your Web browser, such as Internet Explorer, as shown below.

The Google page opens with the Search Bar ready to accept your keyword searches, as shown below.

You can focus your search on categories such as **News, Images** and **Maps,** etc. **Google Maps** and **Google Earth** (a separate program) allow you to see maps and satellite images of places all over the world. **Street View** shows actual photographs of buildings, cars and people. Right-click over the Google window shown above and select **Create Shortcut** and **Yes** to place a clickable icon for Google on your Windows desktop.

Browsing the World Wide Web

When you are connected to a Web site you can move to other Web pages and other Web sites using *clickable links* or *hyperlinks*. As you move the cursor around the screen, when it's over a clickable link the cursor changes to a hand. The link may be a piece of text, a picture or an icon. A text link appears underlined while the cursor is over it, as shown by the **Hotmail** link on the right. In this example, a single click of the link takes you from the MSN Home Page to the Microsoft Hotmail service.

As you move about the Web using clickable links to visit various pages, you may wish to move between pages previously visited. This is achieved by clicking the forward and back buttons found near the top left of the Internet Explorer screen and shown on the right and below.

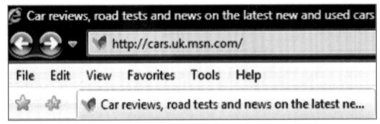

The **File** menu above includes options to **Save** and **Print** a Web page. Clicking **View** above displays options to switch various toolbars on or off (including the Menu Bar itself) and to increase the size of the text on the screen. The **Tools** menu allows you to block *pop-ups* — unsolicited advertisements which can be very annoying when they suddenly appear on the screen. The **Tools** menu also allows you to change your Home Page, i.e. the Web page which automatically appears when you connect to the Internet at the start of a session.

The tab along the bottom right of the screenshot above starting **Car reviews, road tests...** gives details of the current Web page.

Tabbed Browsing

Later versions of Internet Explorer allow you to have several Web sites open simultaneously, represented by tabs across the top of the screen. To switch between Web sites you simply click the tab representing the required Web site.

The group of icons shown below appears near the top right of the Internet Explorer screen.

Reading from left to right, clicking the house icon returns you to your Home Page. The next icon, when coloured orange, represents *RSS feeds*; these are regularly updated items of news and information, relevant to the currently open Web page. The printer icon allows you to print the current Web page on paper and **Page** includes options to save, copy and e-mail a Web page. The **Tools** menu above is very similar to the **Tools** menu on the Menu Bar described on the previous page.

Bookmarking Web Sites

The **Favorites** menu on the previous page and the **Favorites Center** shown below, allow you to bookmark a Web site for future use. To add a Web site to your list of favourite sites, click the overlapping yellow icons shown on the right, then select **Add to Favorites...**.

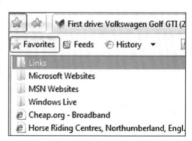

To revisit a site, open **Favorites** and click the name of the site, such as **Horse Riding Centres** shown on the right. The **History** feature shown on the right works in a similar way, allowing you to connect to a Web site from a list of sites which you have visited recently.

Entering Web Addresses

So far we have looked at finding Web pages by searching for relevant keywords such as **American crayfish**, for example. However, you are often given the unique address of a Web site in an advertisement or on headed paper, etc. Most British Web addresses are something like:

www.babanibooks.com

In the above example, **.com** may be replaced by, for example, **.co.uk**, **.net**, or **.org**, depending on the type of organisation owning the Web site. The Web address, such as **www.babanibooks.com**, is entered into the Address Bar in your Web browser, such as Internet Explorer, as shown below:

When you press **Enter**, the characters **http://** are added automatically to complete the full Web address. The required Web site then opens displaying its Home Page.

Mozilla Firefox

Firefox is a Web browser, available as an alternative to Internet Explorer and obtainable as a free download from **www.mozilla.com/firefox/**. Firefox has a reputation for being fast, easy to use and with many innovative features.

Introducing Windows Mail

This is an e-mail program introduced as part of Windows Vista; it is known as an *e-mail client* and replaces Outlook Express provided in Windows XP and earlier versions of Windows.

As shown below, you can launch **Windows Mail** in Vista from the **Start** menu or from the **Start**, **All Programs** menu.

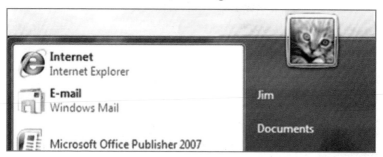

Your computer may already have on icon for Windows Mail on the Vista desktop, as shown on the right. If not you can create an icon by right-clicking **Windows Mail** in the **Start** or **All Programs** menu, then select **Send To** and click **Desktop (create shortcut)**. Double-click this new desktop icon every time you want to launch **Windows Mail**.

Before sending your first e-mail, you need to enter details for your new e-mail *account*, using information provided by your Internet Service Provider such as BT, etc. Some typical information for a BT e-mail account is shown below.

E-mail address:	johnsmith@btinternet.com
Username:	johnsmith
Password:	********
POP3 Incoming mail server:	mail.btinternet.com
SMTP Outgoing mail server:	mail.btinternet.com

Setting Up an E-mail Account in Windows Mail

The first time you try to use **Windows Mail**, the setup wizard starts up and the first dialogue box requires you to enter a **Display name**, such as **John Smith**, for example, as you would like it to appear in the **From** field on the messages you send. After clicking **Next** enter your E-mail address such as **johnsmith@btinternet.com**. After clicking **Next** again enter the details of your incoming and outgoing mail servers. The servers are computers belonging to your Internet Service Provider and handle the e-mails you send and receive. You will need to select from drop-down menus the *type* of servers, such as **POP3** for incoming mail and **SMTP** for outgoing mail. Also enter the *names* of the mail servers, such as **mail@bt.internet.com** for example, as shown in the example at the bottom of page 47.

Finally click **Next** and enter the **E-mail username** and **Password** which you set up with your Internet Service Provider, together with the server details mentioned above.

E-mail Addresses

In order to send someone an e-mail message you must know their unique e-mail address, for example:

> **stella@aol.com**
> **james@msn.com**
> **enquiries@wildlife.org.uk**

The first part of the e-mail address is usually part of your name, followed by the name of the mail server at your company, organisation or Internet Service Provider. The last part of the e-mail address shows the type of organization, such as:

> **.com** commercial company
>
> **.org** non-profit making organisations
>
> **.net** Internet company

Using Windows Mail

Launch **Windows Mail** from the **Start** or **All Programs** menu or by double-clicking its icon on the Desktop. The first screen you see is the **Windows Mail Inbox**.

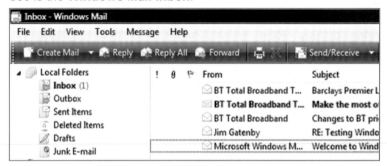

Down the left-hand side of the **Inbox** screen above are the folders for storing messages. Apart from the **Inbox**, the **Outbox** contains messages waiting to be sent, after which they are listed in the **Sent Items** folder. You can delete old e-mails, placing them in the **Deleted Items** folder. Any e-mails which the program decides are "spam" or unsolicited advertising, etc., go in the **Junk E-mail** folder.

Creating an E-mail Message

From the **Inbox** screen select **Create Mail**, as shown below.

The new message window opens and you may wish to click the **Maximise** button shown on the right (in the middle) if you are sending a lengthy message, as shown on the next page. In the **To:** field enter the e-mail address of the person who is to receive the message. You can send messages to more than one person, using semi-colons to separate their addresses.

You are now ready to start entering the text of the message, as shown below. **Windows Mail** has quite a few text formatting features such as different fonts or styles of letters, plus bold, underline, colour and bullets and numbering for lists. You can also use editing features such as "cut and paste".

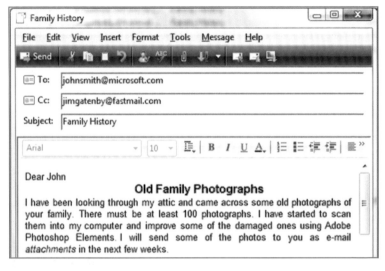

Adding an Attachment

Attachments are files such as photographs or word processing documents, "clipped" onto an e-mail message. Anyone receiving the e-mail together with the attachment can download the attached file and open it on their computer. To attach a file such as a photograph to an e-mail, click the **Attach** icon (shown as a paperclip) on the **Windows Mail** Toolbar as shown below.

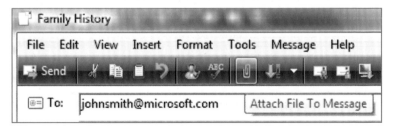

Next the Windows Explorer feature opens, allowing you to locate and select the required picture or document from your computer's hard disc or other location. When you click the **Open** button, the file is attached to the e-mail as shown below in the **Attach** field. You can have several attachments on one e-mail.

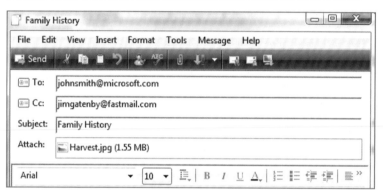

Once the text has been entered and any attachments added, click the **Send** button to get your message on its way.

Receiving an E-mail

When you want to check your mail, open your **Inbox** and click **Send/Receive** as shown below. Extra **Send and Receive** options are also available from the **Tools** menu shown above and below. As an example, I sent the previously described e-mail, **Family History**, to my own e-mail address.

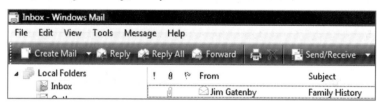

As shown above, the **Family History** message is in my **Inbox** with the attached photo denoted by a paper clip icon.

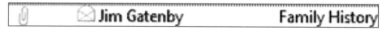

Double-click on the entry for the e-mail as listed in the **Inbox** on the previous page. The message opens for you to read, in its own window as shown below.

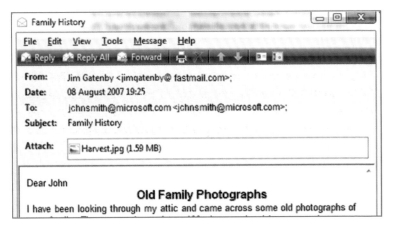

You can reply to the originator after clicking **Reply** or **Reply All** (to include all of the original recipients). The e-mail addresses of the recipients of the reply are filled in automatically.

Double-clicking the entry in the **Attach** field shown above opens the photo or document in its associated program, e.g. the Windows Photo Gallery, Paint or Microsoft Word, where it can be edited, etc., and saved on your hard disc. Or click the file in the messages list and then select **File** and **Save Attachments...** from the toolbar.

5

Windows Revealed

Introduction

Early computers were controlled by entering words like RUN, SAVE and PRINT at the keyboard. These text-based systems were laborious and difficult to use. In the early 1980s the Xerox and Apple companies developed the *Graphical User Interface,* a system of controlling a computer by "pointing and clicking" objects on the screen using a device now known as a *mouse.* The screen objects included *icons,* i.e. small pictures representing tasks such as starting a new page, saving a document as a file on disc or printing on paper, as shown on the right. There were also lists of options or *menus* which popped down on the screen from horizontal menu bars. Information was entered and displayed on the screen in rectangular boxes known as *windows.*

The Apple Macintosh was the first computer to exploit this easy-to-use new system for operating a computer, after which Microsoft developed its own graphical user interface, known as *Windows,* in 1985. There have been several versions of Windows since then and nowadays the majority of new desktop and laptop computers are supplied with a version of Microsoft Windows already installed.

Microsoft Windows is an example of a computer *operating system*, a set of programs used to manage and control all of a computer's functions. The Apple Mac and Linux operating systems are used on a substantial number of computers but Windows is by far the most widely used operating system.

Windows XP, Windows Vista and Windows 7

At the time of writing, most new computers for the home user are supplied with either Windows XP or Windows Vista. Windows XP was released in 2001 and has proved very popular and reliable. Windows Vista, introduced in 2007, is the current flagship version of Windows .

Windows XP and Vista are broadly similar in "look and feel"; I use both systems on a daily basis and, from an ordinary user's point of view, the differences are not great. In my experience, both systems are reliable and easy to use. Windows Vista brought in many advanced 3D graphics features, known as Windows Aero, as shown in the example below.

These Vista graphics features demand more computing power. While most new computers (other than netbooks) should be able to run Vista and all of its graphics features, some older machines do not have the power unless they can be upgraded.

For the owner of an older computer wishing to upgrade from Windows XP to Windows Vista, one option was to buy a new, more powerful computer; alternatively you could upgrade an older machine, e.g. by fitting extra memory and a new graphics card, etc. (These topics are discussed in more detail in Chapter 9). Consequently many users have decided to stay with Windows XP rather than upgrade to Vista; in addition many new machines are still supplied with Windows XP pre-installed.

Compatibility Issues

When a new operating system like Windows Vista is introduced, some existing software, i.e. programs, may not work with the new system; similarly hardware devices like printers may not be compatible. This may be because the manufacturers of the device have not yet developed software, called *device drivers,* which enable a device to work with an operating system. Eventually suitable driver software may be available, usually from the device manufacturer's Web site. However, for an older device such as a printer, the manufacturer may decide not to develop suitable device driver software. So changing to Vista could mean that some of your existing hardware and software could no longer be used and would need to be replaced. In this case, the benefits of upgrading to Vista may not justify the extra expense, at least until it was time to buy a new computer.

The Netbook Phenomenon

Another reason for the refusal of Windows XP to be totally eclipsed by Vista is the recent phenomenal success of the new breed of small, cheap *netbook* computers; in spite of their relatively low specification they can still run Windows XP quite comfortably. Vista would demand too much computing power and might be too expensive for these cut-price minis.

Windows 7

This is the latest version of Windows, successor to Windows Vista and discussed in more detail later in this chapter.

Functions of the Windows Operating System

Some of the main tasks carried out by the Windows operating system are:

- Starting up and shutting down the computer.

- Controlling the screen display of windows, icons, etc.

- Managing the saving and printing of documents as *files*.

- Installing, running and removing *applications,* i.e. programs used for tasks such as word processing, drawing, spreadsheets and editing photographs.

- Installing, setting up and removing hardware such as printers and network devices like modems, routers, etc.

- Carrying out "housekeeping" tasks such as deleting files, preparing and maintaining the hard disc drive.

- Managing connections to networks such as a small home or local area network (LAN) and the Internet.

- Tailoring a computer, through the Ease of Access Center, to help someone with *special needs*, such as impaired vision or reduced manual dexterity.

- Providing security software, such as *Windows Firewall*, to prevent hackers from accessing the computer.

- Downloading the latest software updates, from Microsoft via the Internet, e.g. for improved security.

- Providing online help and support.

The notes which follow are based on Windows Vista; however, Windows XP is broadly similar and users of XP should find virtually all of the material relevant to their system. The main difference is that some of the more exotic Vista graphics features are not present in Windows XP.

The Windows Desktop

After the computer has started up, you are presented with the Windows Desktop. The Windows Vista Desktop is shown below.

Various backgrounds are available in the **Personalization** feature in the Windows **Control Panel**, discussed shortly. Down the left-hand side above are icons for various programs such as Google Earth, for example. Double-click an icon to quickly launch the program. You can place icons for your own regularly-used programs on the desktop, as discussed later in this book. On the right of the desktop is the **Sidebar**, an optional panel displaying *gadgets* such as a calendar and the latest news.

The horizontal bar across the bottom of the screen is called the **Taskbar**, with the circular **Start** orb on the left and the

Quick Launch toolbar icons to the right of the **Start** orb.

In the middle of the **Taskbar**, the names and icons of currently running programs are displayed; clicking these enables you to switch between tasks.

On the bottom right of the **Taskbar** is the **System Tray**, also known as the **Notification Area**. This group of icons can be expanded as shown below, by clicking the arrow on the left.

The four icons on the right above appear as standard; these icons represent the **Windows Sidebar**, the Internet connection, the speaker volume and the clock. Other icons appear after you have installed new hardware or software. The icons in the **System Tray** can be used to find information, alter settings or switch features on or off. Allowing the cursor to hover over an icon in the **System Tray** gives information about the icon, as for the Internet connection icon shown on the left and right below.

Right-clicking an icon in the **System Tray** opens a pop-up menu relevant to the icon, as shown below on the right after right-clicking the Internet connection icon. Clicking **Network and Sharing Center** on the menu, for example, opens up a window allowing you to check the status of your Internet connection and alter various Internet settings.

The Start Menu

Click the **Start** orb at the bottom left of the screen as shown on the right. The Start Menu appears as shown in the extract below. This is the main method for launching programs in Microsoft Windows; all the programs installed on the computer can be accessed from the sub-menu which appears when you click **All Programs** as shown below. Frequently-used programs such as **Internet Explorer** and programs you've used recently appear in the left-hand panel of the Start Menu. As mentioned earlier, you can also launch a program by double-clicking an icon on the Windows Desktop.

Searching for Files and Folders

The **Start Search** bar at the bottom left of the Start Menu enables you to find any file or folder saved on your computer and on the Internet, after entering its name or part of its name, as shown on the right. This particular search would find any files or folders

containing the word **cats** in the file or folder name.

On the right of the Start Menu on the previous page are options to launch various Windows features such as **Recent Items** to retrieve documents you have been working on lately. **Network** allows you to check any computers and routers you may have connected to a home network and there is also a link to Windows **Help and Support**.

The Computer Window

Listed on the Start Menu on the previous page is the word **Computer**, also shown in the small menu extract on the right. In this case the word **Computer** refers to a window which opens up to show all the disc resources on the computer. The same feature is present in Windows XP and known as **My Computer**.

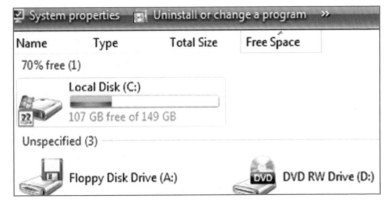

The **Computer** Window is useful in a number of ways. In the example on the previous page you can see that the hard disc drive **(C:)** has **107 GB free of 149 GB**. (The terms gigabytes or GB are explained in Chapter 9.)

If you plug in a USB flash drive (also known as a *pen drive*), this will appear as another disc drive in the **Computer**  window, as shown for the **Kingston** *Data Traveler* above.

Now right-click any device in the **Computer** window and select **Properties** from the menu which pops up. In this case the **Kingston** flash drive was right-clicked, showing that there is still plenty of storage space left on this particular drive.

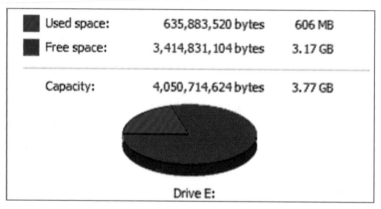

The **Computer** window is particularly useful for moving between folders on your hard disc. For example on my **C:** drive there is a hierarchy of folders and sub-folders as shown below. After double-clicking the **C:** drive in the **Computer** window as shown on page 60, keep double-clicking sub-folders till you reach the file you want.

In the **Computer** Window below, some of the chapters of this book are listed in the top half as files in the Adobe Acrobat PDF format and in the lower half as Microsoft Publisher files. From the Address Bar at the top of the **Computer** window, you can see that these document files are stored in a folder called **Getting Started Publisher**, which is a sub-folder of **Getting Started**, which is itself a sub-folder of the **Colour Series** folder.

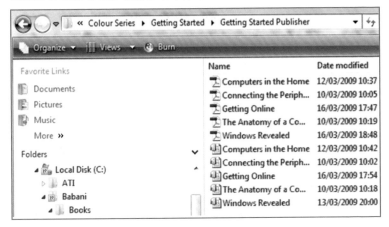

Opening a File from the Computer Window

Once you've double-clicked your way down the hierarchy of folders and sub-folders to find the document or file that you want, double-click the file name to open the document in its associated program. For example, if you double-click a file originally created in Word, the word processor program will start up with your document already open. If the file is a photo or picture, right-click the file name in the **Computer** window, then select **Open With** from the menu which pops up. Now

click the name of the program you wish to open the file in, such as **Paint**, for example, as shown above to the right.

The Control Panel

This is another feature listed on the Start Menu shown on page 59 and in the small extract on the right. Click **Control Panel** and a window opens in one of two optional formats, **Classic View** (shown below) or **Control Panel Home**. The **Control Panel**  provides a huge range of software tools for altering the settings on your computer, adding and deleting hardware and software and keeping it running efficiently.

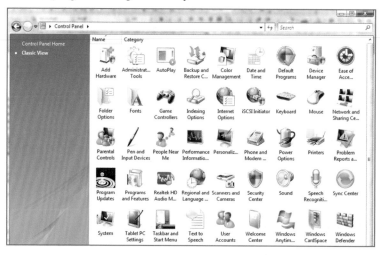

The **Control Panel Home** view presents the tools grouped in a number of categories, such as **Security** shown on the right, rather than as separate icons as shown in the **Classic View** above. Two links at the top left of the **Control Panel** allow you to switch between the two views, as shown on the right.

To launch a tool from the **Classic View** of the **Control Panel**, double-click the appropriate icon. In the **Control Panel Home** view it's simply a case of clicking the categories until you find the required feature or tool. A few samples from **Classic View** of the **Control Panel** are given below:

Ease of Access Center

The Ease of Access Center allows you to adjust settings on your computer to help with special needs such as impaired vision and restricted mobility. This subject is discussed in more detail in Chapter 6, Windows Help for Users with Special Needs.

Printers

Double-clicking this icon shows the printer driver software installed on your computer, allows you to add a printer and alter printer settings as well as cancel a job which is being printed. A printer can be designated as the default printer.

Personaliz...

Personalization lets you alter the appearance of Windows features such as a choice of desktop backgrounds, the colours used for displaying windows, the mouse settings and the screen resolution (i.e. the number of pixels or dots).

Device Manager

The **Device Manager** lists all of the devices such as disc drives, keyboard, mouse, monitor, network adaptors, USB ports, etc., and allows you to check if they are working correctly. You can also update the device driver software, uninstall the device driver software or disable the device.

Windows Firewall

The **Windows Firewall** is intended to prevent hackers and malicious software from invading your computer. Double-clicking this icon allows you to switch the firewall on or off and also make exceptions to allow access by people you trust.

Windows Applications

The previous pages discussed some of the features in Windows used to control and manage the computer; this type of software is often referred to as *systems software* and also *utilities*.

Programs used to achieve a non-computing end result of your own, such as writing letters, drawing a picture or editing a photograph, are known as *applications*. Another example of an application would be a genealogy program to help trace your family history. Such programs would normally be bought as boxed packages and installed on your hard disc from a CD or DVD (as discussed in Chapter 7 Installing and Using Software). However, when the Windows Vista or XP operating systems are installed on a computer, they also include several built-in applications of their own. Some of these Windows applications are discussed on the next few pages.

Windows Paint

This is a drawing program in which pictures can be created, edited, rotated, resized and saved in various formats, including the JPEG photographic format. **Paint** is launched by clicking the **Start** orb, then **All Programs**, **Accessories** and **Paint**.

The Windows Media Player

The **Windows Media Player** is launched by clicking the **Start** button followed by **All Programs** and **Windows Media Player**. This program allows you to play CDs and DVDs and manage libraries of digital music and videos stored on your hard disc. The **Media Player** can be used to "rip", i.e. copy, music and video files from CD to your hard disc; also "burn", i.e. write files onto a CD or DVD. Music can be organised in categories or alternatively playlists of your favourite tracks can be created and saved. (Some early CD drives cannot write or "burn" data onto a DVD; for this you need a "combi" drive, usually designated **DVD RW**. This will also read and write ordinary CDs.)

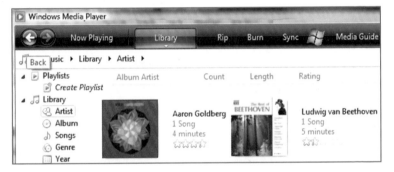

Across the bottom of the **Window Media Player** there is a toolbar (shown below) with buttons (reading from left to right) to *shuffle* the order of tunes in a playlist, *repeat* a piece of music and then the usual *stop*, *previous*, *play*, *next* and *fast forward*. Finally on the right are the *mute* and *volume control* buttons.

The **Media Guide** allows you to access an online store and buy music, DVDs, etc., and tune in to numerous Internet radio stations.

The Windows Photo Gallery

With a home computer you can save, edit, polish and print your pictures in the comfort of your own home. You don't need to be an expert to get good results — it's much easier and cheaper than traditional photography using film.

Windows Vista has its own built-in software, the Windows Photo Gallery, for managing and editing photos from a digital camera. (Windows XP has the Windows Picture and Fax Viewer).

When you buy a digital camera the package should include a cable to connect the camera to a USB port on your computer. As it's a USB connection you can plug in the camera while the computer is up and running.

The camera is detected and the **AutoPlay** window appears, giving you options to **Import pictures** or **View pictures** in Windows. After you've imported the pictures to your computer, they can be edited and saved on your hard disc or "burned" to a CD or DVD for a more secure archive. (A collection of precious family photographs needs to be

backed up onto a secure *permanent* storage medium — unfortunately the hard disc is not totally secure since it may be accidentally wiped or damaged, as some people have already discovered.)

Right-click an icon of a photo in the **Computer** window as
discussed earlier, then click **Open With** and **Windows Photo
Gallery**. The **Photo Gallery** opens to display the photograph as
shown below.

The Menu Bar across the top of the **Picture
Gallery** contains a **File** menu with options to
Make a Copy, **Delete** and **Rename** a file.
The **Fix** menu shown on the right contains
tools to edit and improve images. There are
also options on the Menu Bar to **Print**, **E-
mail** and **Burn** a photograph to a CD/DVD.

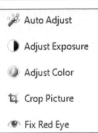

Across the bottom of the **Photo Gallery**
there are icons, shown below, to change the display size of a
photo, start a slide show or select the next or previous image.
The red cross on the right deletes the photo.

Other Windows Features

There are many other programs included within Windows XP and Windows Vista; several of these are discussed in more detail in later chapters of this book. These include the **Internet Explorer** Web page browser and the Vista e-mail program, known as **Windows Mail**. Windows XP uses **Outlook Express** as its e-mail program or *client*. (A client in computing terminology is the name given to a program used by an individual computer to access a program on a network *server* computer).

Notepad and **Wordpad** are two more programs provided as part of Windows XP and Vista and are both launched after clicking **Start**, **All Programs** and **Accessories**. **Notepad** is a basic program for entering, editing, saving and printing text. **Wordpad** is a more complex program containing many of the text formatting features of a word processor such as Microsoft Word.

The **Accessories** menu contains a wealth of other small applications and utilities. These include **Ease of Access**, which enables you to adjust the settings of a computer to help people with special needs. **Ease of Access** is discussed in Chapter 6. The **Snipping Tool** in Vista enables you to capture a section of the screen, add notes to the image and save it on disc as a **JPEG** picture file. With the addition of a microphone, the **Sound Recorder** allows you to make recordings and save them on your hard disc.

The **Systems Tools** sub-menu on the **Accessories** menu hosts a number of utilities for keeping a computer running efficiently, including **Disk Cleanup**, **Disk Defragmenter** and **System Restore**. Finally there is **Windows Update** which provides the latest Windows software modifications and improvements from Microsoft, delivered to your computer from the Internet. **Windows Update** is launched from **Start** and **All Programs**. Chapter 8 covers **System Tools** and **Windows Update** in more detail.

Windows 7

At the time of writing this book in Spring 2009, Vista is the current version of Microsoft Windows; the previous version, Windows XP, is still going strong and being supplied on many new computers, especially laptops and netbooks, as discussed earlier. Windows 7 is the successor to Vista and is currently in the final stages of testing. Trial versions of Windows 7, known as *beta test* software, have been available as a free Internet download for some time. The beta version may not be fully representative of the final edition of Windows 7 released for sale, but some first impressions are:

- Most of the main Windows features discussed earlier in this chapter are still present.

- The overall layout and structure of Windows 7 is broadly similar to Windows XP and Vista.

- A simpler, cleaner and more stylish desktop.

- Fewer gadgets and no sidebar as used in Vista.

- A redesigned Taskbar with bigger icons, as shown below.

- An option to operate with a touch-sensitive screen.

- Less emphasis on Vista Aero graphics features, so Windows 7 should be less demanding of computing power than Windows Vista.

- Windows 7 has been stated to run faster than Windows Vista.

- A version suitable for relatively low specification netbook computers is thought to be planned.

6

Windows Help for Users with Special Needs

Introduction

Windows Vista contains a number of **Ease of Access** features designed to help common impairments such as:

- Poor Eyesight
- Reduced Manual Dexterity
- Impaired Hearing

The **Ease of Access** menu is launched by selecting **Start**, **All Programs**, **Accessories** and **Ease of Access**. (You may need to scroll down the list of programs in the **All**

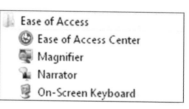

Programs menu in the left-hand panel of the **Start** menu until **Accessories** is visible.)

The next section looks at the Vista **Ease of Access** features, shown in the menu on the right above.

The **Magnifier**, **Narrator** and **On-Screen Keyboard** in the Vista **Ease of Access** menu shown above are also present in the Windows XP **Accessibility** menu obtained by selecting **Start**, **All Programs, Accessories** and **Accessibility**.

Some users may require more specialised accessibility software and equipment than the tools available in Windows. As discussed shortly, further help can be found by entering keywords into an Internet search program such as Google.

The Ease of Access Center

This feature can be launched in several ways. For example, click **Start**, **Control Panel** and double-click the icon shown on the right in the **Control Panel** in **Classic View**. Alternatively you can open the **Ease of Access Center** from **Control Panel Home** as shown below:

Ease of Access Center

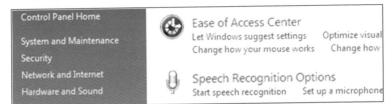

Next select **Ease of Access Center**, as shown above, to see the full list of accessibility tools.

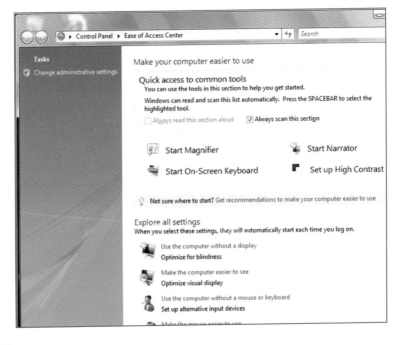

The Magnifier

As shown in the previous window, you can go directly to any of the various **Ease of Access** tools, such as the **Magnifier**, for example. The **Magnifier** produces an enlarged display of the text and graphics around the current cursor position.

The Narrator

The **Narrator** reads out aloud the contents of the windows displayed on the screen, including titles, menu options, features such as buttons and check boxes, and keys as they are typed.

The On-Screen Keyboard

If you find a normal keyboard difficult to use, you can "type" by using the mouse to click the letters on the image of a keyboard on the screen.

The above features are discussed in more detail shortly.

High Contrast

This option makes the screen easier to read by increasing the contrast on colours. **High Contrast** is switched on and off by simultaneously pressing down **Alt** + left **Shift** + **PRINT SCREEN** (may be marked **Prt Sc** on your keyboard).

Finding Out Your Own Special Needs

If you are not sure which tools you need to help you, the **Ease of Access Center** allows you to select your particular needs from several lists of impairments. Then a list of recommended settings is produced which you may choose to switch on if you wish. To start entering any difficulties you may have, click on **Get recommendations to make your computer easier to use**, halfway down the **Ease of Access Center** window, as shown below and on the previous page.

Not sure where to start? Get recommendations to make your computer easier to use

You are presented with a series of statements under the headings **Eyesight, Dexterity, Hearing, Speech** and **Reasoning**. Each statement is preceded by a check box, which you can tick by clicking with the mouse if it applies to you. For example, the **Eyesight** statements are shown below:

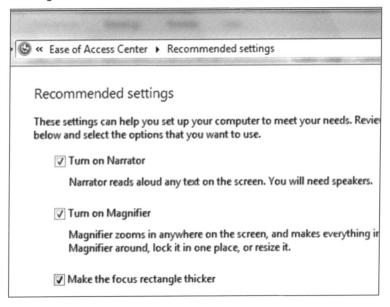

After you click **Next**, the investigation of your needs continues with the statements on **Dexterity, Hearing, Speech** and **Reasoning**. Finally you are presented with a list of recommended settings which you may choose to switch on by clicking to tick the check box, as shown below:

The list of **Recommended settings** shown previously may also include options to change the colour and size of the mouse pointers as shown below:

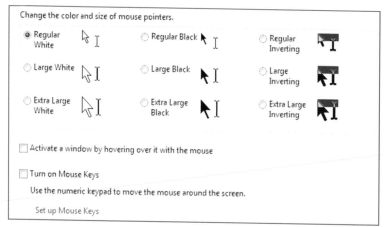

Other options include **Turn on Sticky Keys**. Some keyboard "shortcuts" require three keys on the keyboard to be pressed simultaneously. **Sticky Keys** allow these operations to be reduced to a single key press.

Turn on Mouse Keys shown above enables the numeric keypad (on the right of the keyboard) and also the arrow keys, to move the mouse pointer around the screen.

When you've finished selecting your **Ease of Access** recommended settings, click **Apply** and **Save** near the bottom of the screen. From now on, each time you start the computer, your chosen features, such as the **Magnifier** or the **On-Screen Keyboard**, will start up automatically.

At the bottom of the list of **Ease of Access** recommendations is a clickable link to a Web site giving further information about organisations and products intended to make computers easier to use.

Learn about additional assistive technologies online

The Magnifier

If you are finding the text and graphics difficult to read, you can enlarge the area around the current cursor position by switching on the **Magnifier** in the **Ease of Access Center**. Select **Start, Control Panel** and **Ease of Access**. Then click **Start Magnifier** in the **Ease of Access Center** shown below.

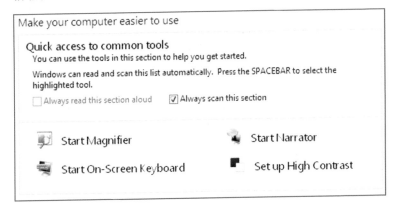

The magnified text and graphics appear in a separate window at the top of the screen, as shown below.

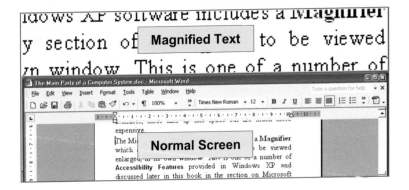

The **Magnifier** also appears as a minimised icon on the Windows Vista Taskbar as shown below.

If you click this icon, the **Magnifier** window opens, presenting a number of settings which can be adjusted. These include the **Scale factor** for the magnification, up to a maximum of **16x**.

The magnified area can be placed at the **Top**, **Left**, **Right** or **Bottom** of the screen, using the **Dock position** option shown on the right. The **Magnifier** dialogue box window shown on the right can be set to start up either minimised or full size.

The **Magnifier** can be switched off by clicking the **Close** icon in the top right-hand corner of the **Magnifier** window shown above Alternatively, right-click over the **Magnifier** Taskbar icon and click **Close** off the menu which pops up, as shown on the right.

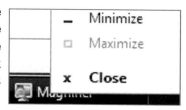

The On-Screen Keyboard

Click **Start On-Screen Keyboard** in the **Ease of Access Center** shown on page 76. The keyboard image immediately pops up on the screen, as shown below:

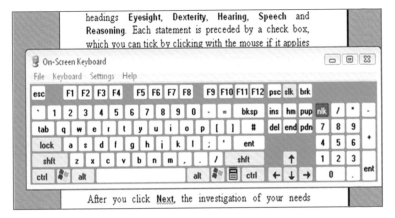

There is also an icon for the **On-Screen Keyboard** on the Vista Taskbar at the bottom of the screen.

Place the cursor where you want to begin typing and simply point to and click the required letters and characters. Upper or lower case letters are obtained by clicking one of the on-screen **shft** keys. The **On-Screen Keyboard** can be moved to a convenient position by dragging in the Title Bar to the right of the words **On-Screen Keyboard**.

To switch off the **On-Screen Keyboard**, click the **Close** icon in the top right-hand corner of the keyboard or right-click the Taskbar icon and click the **Close** option on the menu which pops-up.

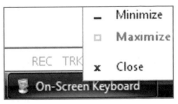

The Narrator

If your computer has the sound facility set up, you can use the **Narrator** to give a spoken commentary as you work. The **Narrator** tells you what keys you've pressed and also reads out details of any windows you've opened, including menu options and features such as buttons and check boxes. The **Narrator** is launched by clicking **Start Narrator** in the **Ease of Access Center**, as shown on page 76.

After a few seconds the **Narrator** window appears, allowing you to make various adjustments to the settings. There is also a **Microsoft Narrator** icon on the Vista Taskbar.

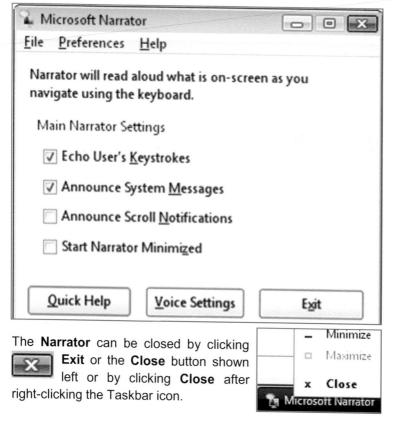

The **Narrator** can be closed by clicking **Exit** or the **Close** button shown left or by clicking **Close** after right-clicking the Taskbar icon.

Further Help

There are many companies and organisations offering more specialist help than is provided by the tools available within Windows Vista, just discussed. For example, alternative input devices are available for sufferers of illnesses such as Parkinson's Disease or Cerebral Palsy. As mentioned earlier, there is a link, shown below, at the end of the **Ease of Access Recommended settings** in Windows Vista.

> Learn about additional assistive technologies online

Clicking this link enables you to access a wide range of information on assistive or accessibility issues. There are also links to the Web sites of companies providing specialist devices, such as, for example, the **Head Mounted Mousing Alternative** link below.

> **Tracker 2000 - Head Mounted Mousing Alternative** by Madentec Limited
> "Great for Those with Limited Mobility" **More**

You can also carry out your own Internet search for help by entering relevant keywords, such as **disability computer technology** or **special needs computer equipment** or **computer accessibility** into a search engine such as Google.

Click on any of the links (which appear underlined in the list of search results) to view the relevant Web site.

7

Installing and Using Software

Introduction

Microsoft Office 2007 is a suite of several programs based around the word processor Microsoft Word and the spreadsheet Microsoft Excel. These are part of the world's leading office automation software and are discussed shortly; while they are powerful enough for sophisticated business users they are also very user-friendly and suitable for the most inexperienced home user. Microsoft Word can be used for anything from a simple document to a 300-page book including text and pictures. In fact I have used Word to produce nearly 30 books, including most of the "Babani Older Generation" series.

There are several versions of Microsoft Office, but most home and small business users should find the Office Home and Student 2007 edition meets most of their needs. The programs included with Office Home and Student are **Word**, **Excel**, **OneNote** and **PowerPoint**. **OneNote** is used for collecting and organising all sorts of information in different forms such as text, pictures and video clips. PowerPoint is used for creating slides of text and graphics to illustrate talks and presentations. This chapter concentrates on Word 2007 and Excel 2007.

Office Home and Student 2007 can be purchased for under £60 and may be legally installed on up to 3 computers. This price is for an *upgrade* from an earlier *qualifying* version of Microsoft software.

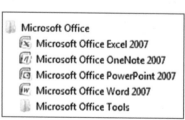

81

Installing Microsoft Office 2007

The Product Key

On the back of an inner plastic case in the Office package is the PRODUCT KEY label. The product key is your licence to install the software – it's used to validate and activate the software so that it can be used on your computer. It's worth making a copy of the 25-character key and storing it in a safe place. You might have a technical problem later and need to re-install the Office software – well-nigh impossible without the product key.

During the installation process you will be asked to enter your 25-character product key. If you don't enter a product key you will only be able to use the software for a limited time, e.g. 30 days.

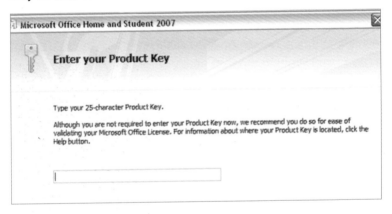

If the product key is genuine, a green tick appears and you then click **Continue** to carry on with the installation. After choosing to either **Upgrade** or **Customize** you are presented with a window showing the **Progress** of the installation as a percentage. Finally you are informed that the software has been successfully installed and you can, if you wish, click the **Go to Office Online** link to get updates, help and online services.

As with many software installations, you need to restart the computer before using the software for the first time.

Activation

Microsoft Office has to be *activated*, a process intended to prevent software being installed on more than the permitted number of computers. (Office Home & Student 2007 is licensed for up to 3 installations). You are given the choice to activate over the Internet or by telephone. Internet activation occurs automatically; telephone activation requires an assurance that you are not installing too many copies of the software. If you don't activate your copy of Office 2007 you will only be able to use the software for a limited number of sessions.

Launching the Programs

At the end of the installation process you will find entries for **Microsoft Office**, including **Word** and **Excel**, in the **All Programs** menu accessed via the **Start** orb in the bottom left-hand corner of the screen as shown below.

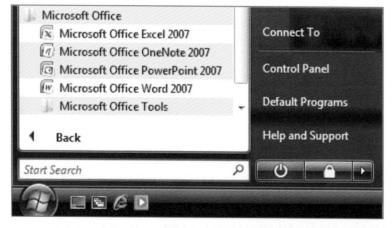

Any of the component programs of Office Home & Student 2007 can now be launched by clicking their entry in the **All Programs** menu shown above. As shown on the next page, a new, radically different "user interface" has been introduced in Microsoft Office 2007 and this has been applied to the Word, Excel and PowerPoint programs.

The Tabbed Ribbon

In Office 2007 the traditional drop-down menus such as **File**, **Edit** and **View**, etc., have been replaced by a *tabbed ribbon* as shown below. Ribbons are used in Word, Excel and PowerPoint.

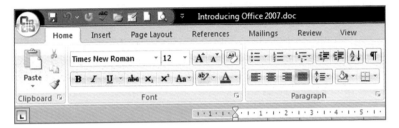

All of the usual tools are still available – it's just that they are presented in a different layout. On the ribbon there are various tabs such as **Home**, **Insert** and **Page Layout**, as shown above. Icons and tools for particular tasks are grouped together, such as the **Font** group for changing the style and size of letters. The text formatting tools such as indentation, centring, justification and line spacing are displayed in the **Paragraph** group shown above.

One of the most striking features of the ribbon is that as you change to a different task, the tools on the ribbon change automatically. For example, if you select a picture or image so that it's highlighted in a Word document, the **Format** tab with **Picture Tools** above it, appears as shown below. Clicking this tab displays a complete set of tools for formatting a picture. An extract from the ribbon displaying the **Picture Tools** on the **Format** tab is shown below.

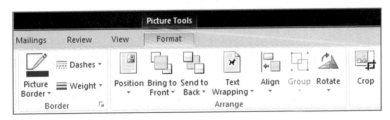

The Office Button

If you allow the cursor to hover over the **Office Button** (shown on the right) in the top left-hand corner of the screen, a small help window appears, as shown below. The **Office Button** is used for major tasks such as saving and printing a Word document or Excel spreadsheet, as well as for opening a new document.

If you need extra help at any time, press the **F1** key near the top left-hand side of the keyboard. For example, if you press **F1** while the cursor is over the **Office Button**, the **Word Help** window appears giving further support.

Clicking the **Office Button** displays a drop-down menu similar to the **File** menu found in previous versions of Word and Excel. The **Office Button** menu displays the options for major tasks, such as saving and printing your work and starting a new document. The **Office Button** menu is shown on the next page, open at the **Save As** option.

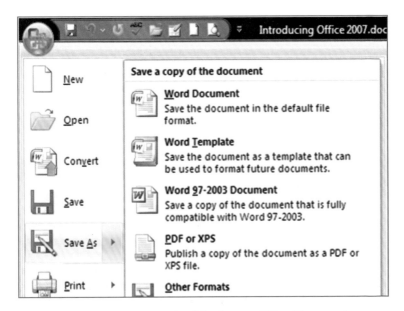

Saving Documents in Various File Formats

The **Save As** option in Word 2007 can be used to save documents in a number of different file formats, as shown below. These include:

Word Document (.docx)

The **.docx** format was introduced in Word 2007. To read **.docx** files into earlier versions of Word, download the Office Compatibility Pack from Microsoft Office Online.

Word 97-2003 Document

Save in this format if you want to create documents which can be opened in earlier versions of Word. Conversely, Word 2007 can open documents created in earlier versions of Word.

PDF (Portable Document Format)

This is a universal format which can be read on any type of computer, using a program called Adobe Reader, available as a free download from the Adobe Web site at **www.adobe.co.uk**.

Introducing Word 2007

Word processing is one of the most frequently used applications of computers and Microsoft Word is the undisputed world leader. The modern word processor is capable of creating all sorts of documents, such as:

- Letters to friends and relatives
- Reports including tables and graphs
- A newsletter for a club or parish magazine
- College reports such as a thesis or dissertation
- Leaflets and flyers including artwork and pictures, with text in various shapes, known as WordArt, as shown below.

Composting News

- A novel or book (such as this one) as shown below.

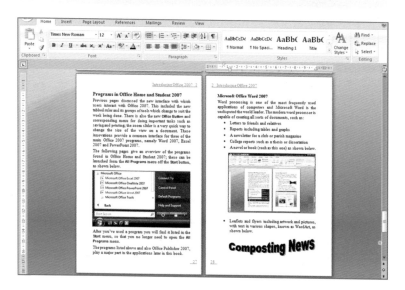

Advantages of Word Processors

Word processors are far more versatile than the traditional typewriter; they are easy to use and allow anyone to produce professional-looking documents. Some of the advantages of the word processor are as follows:

- Corrections can be made on the screen before printing on paper, so there is no evidence of any alterations. Several copies can easily be printed.

- Documents are saved on disc and can be retrieved later. This allows a document to be used again, perhaps with small changes such as a new date. There is no need to retype the whole document.

- Text can be *edited* more easily – whole blocks of text can be inserted, deleted or moved to a new position in the document.

- The *Find and Replace* feature enables a word (or group of words) to be exchanged for another word (or words), wherever they occur in a document.

- Text can be formatted with effects such as bold and italic and in various fonts or styles of lettering, such as the Algerian font shown below.

ALGERIAN

- The layout of the page can easily be changed or with text set in tables or newspaper-style columns.

- Modern word processors contain many additional features such as spelling and grammar checkers, a thesaurus and a word count facility.

Introducing Excel 2007

Excel is the world's leading spreadsheet program; it is designed to work on tables of figures, reducing long and complex calculations to simple point-and-click operations using a mouse. Excel 2007 is operated using a new ribbon interface, very similar to the one used in Word 2007 as described earlier in this chapter.

Although Excel is mainly used for calculations, it can also be used as a type of database for keeping text-based records and sorting them into order. I have used Excel for storing hundreds of names and addresses; these are then input into the mail merge facility in Microsoft Word for the automatic printing of address labels, saving a huge amount of time.

Recalculation

The spreadsheet allows you to speculate on the effect of possible changes, such as an increase in the price of petrol. These changes can be fed into the spreadsheet, which automatically recalculates all of the totals, etc., affected by the change. The *recalculation* feature is one of the main advantages of spreadsheet programs and can save many hours of work compared with traditional methods of calculation using pencil and paper or electronic calculators.

Graphs and Charts

Apart from the ability to perform the whole range of mathematical calculations, data can be presented in the form of pie charts, bar charts and line graphs, etc.

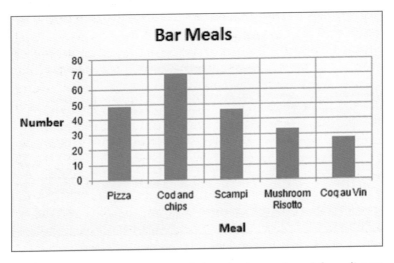

Both the spreadsheet itself and the charts produced from it can be imported into documents in a word processor. This feature is useful, for example, when producing a report on sales performance in a business.

Good Housekeeping

Introduction

Modern computers are very reliable if treated with care; for a good many years I've had three or more budget computers up and running at home and there have been no major problems. However, there are steps you can take to keep your computer running reliably and also safe from external threats. Normal running of your computer creates a lot of debris in the form of redundant and disorganized files and so your hard disc can benefit from a bit of care and attention from time to time.

Unfortunately computer crime is on the increase and there are plenty of highly skilled hackers using the Internet who may try to get hold of your personal information, such as bank account details. In addition there is the constant threat of viruses or malicious software (*malware*), spread to your computer from the Internet and e-mails. Malware is software which may cause damage to your computer's files or theft of your data and inconvenience to yourself.

You might let children or grandchildren "play" on your computer or "improve" it by changing a few settings or installing some software of their own. While most children are sensible and many are brilliant computer whiz-kids, as a former teacher I know there are some children who can wreak havoc, either accidentally or deliberately. If you're using a computer for serious work, whether business, social or charitable, it's a good idea if that machine is kept separate from any computer used by other people for entertainment.

This chapter describes some simple steps you can take to keep your computer running at its best level of performance; they don't require any special skill, won't cost a lot of money and most will only take a few minutes.

Disk Cleanup

During normal running, your computer creates a lot of temporary files on the hard disc. When you browse the Internet, the content of Web pages is temporarily saved so the site can be viewed more quickly next time. When using a program like Word 2007, more temporary files are created. These take up disc space and if ignored for a long time may cause the computer to run slowly.

To remove these redundant files cluttering up your hard disc, run **Disk Cleanup**, once a week say, by selecting **Start**, **All Programs**, **Accessories**, **System Tools** and **Disk Cleanup**.

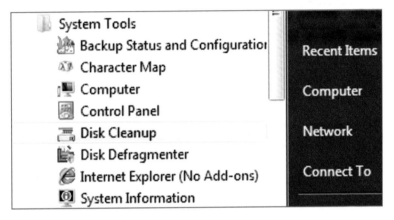

After you've used **Disk Cleanup** once, in future the program can be launched straightaway from the main **Start** menu. A window opens giving you the chance to clean up just your own files or the files of all users of the computer. After making a selection, you choose the drive you wish to clean up – usually drive **(C:)**. **Disk Cleanup** then takes a few minutes to calculate how much disc space can **be** saved by deleting unnecessary files.

After calculating the potential gain in recovered disc space, the unnecessary files are listed, as shown below.

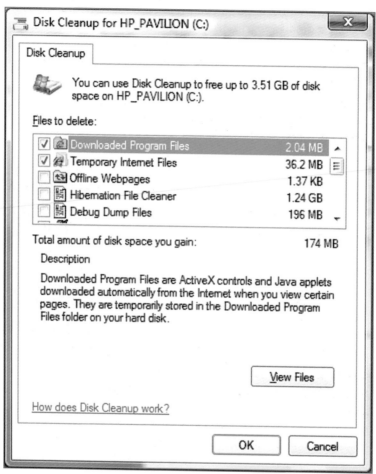

When you click on an entry, such as **Temporary Internet Files**, the purpose of the files is explained in the **Description** panel as well as guidance on the effects of removing them.

Decide which files to delete and click their check boxes so that a tick appears. The amount of free disc space which can be gained is displayed in the window shown on the previous page. When you've marked which files are to be deleted, click **OK** and the window shown below appears.

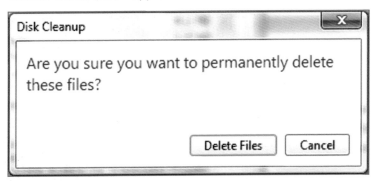

Click the **Delete Files** button shown above to complete the cleanup operation.

You can quickly check the free space on your hard disc by clicking the **Start** orb, then click **Computer** off the **Start** menu. The extract from the **Computer** window on the right shows that the hard disc drive **(C:)** initially had **24.0GB** free space. After running **Disk Cleanup**, the amount of free space increased to **24.2GB**. Much greater savings of several

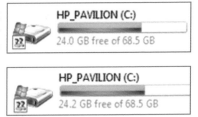

gigabytes can be made using **Disk Cleanup**. For example, you might delete the **Hibernation File**, shown on the previous page, if you don't use the hibernation power setting on your computer. Also by deleting **Temporary files** stored in a **TEMP** folder and not modified in the last week. (Viewable after scrolling down the **Disk Cleanup** window shown on the previous page).

Using Disk Defragmenter

After you've been using your computer for a while, many files will have been repeatedly modified and resaved. The original files and the changes may become separated, scattered about the hard disc in different places. This will impair the performance of the computer when it tries to open a file which is spread around many different locations; *defragmentation* is a process which rearranges the files on the hard disc to make the computer run more efficiently. In Windows Vista, the **Disk Defragmenter** program is scheduled to run automatically. Alternatively it can be launched by clicking the **Start** orb then selecting **All Programs**, **Accessories**, **System Tools** and **Disk Defragmenter**.

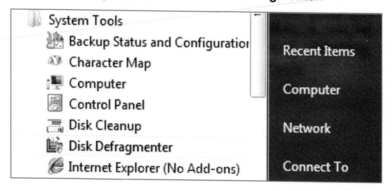

After you've used **Disk Defragmenter** the first time, the program can be launched in future by clicking its name, which by now will be listed on the **Start** menu.

The **Disk Defragmenter** window opens, as shown on the next page. In this particular example, the **Disk Defragmenter** program has been scheduled to run once a week, but you can change this if you wish after clicking **Modify schedule....**

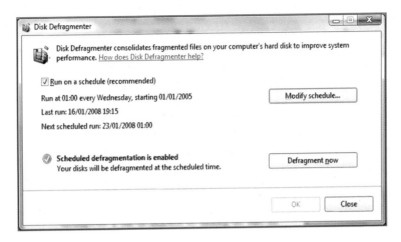

Please also note in the **Disk Defragmenter** window above, the **Defragment now** button allows you to manually start an immediate defragmentation whenever you think it might be beneficial. Select the drive you wish to defragment, usually **(C:)** then click the **Defragment** button.

The defragmentation process may take several minutes or a few hours, depending on the size and state of the hard disc. Fortunately you can continue to use the computer while the **Disk Defragmenter** program is running.

Regular Servicing

It's recommended that, in order to keep your computer running efficiently, **Disk Cleanup** and **Disk Defragmenter** are run regularly – at least once a week, especially if the computer is heavily used. If the computer appears to be running slowly for no obvious reason, it may be worth carrying out a manual defragmentation.

The Windows Security Center

You can carry out a check of all the security features in Windows Vista by launching the **Windows Security Center**. Click **Start**, **Control Panel** and double-click the **Security Center** icon as shown on the right. You are recommended to make sure that the main security features are either switched **On** or marked **OK** as shown below.

Security Center

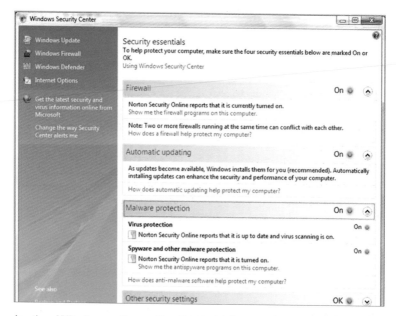

In the **Windows Security Center** shown above, each of the main features, **Firewall**, **Automatic updating** and **Malware protection**, etc., has been expanded to give more information. This is done by clicking the downward pointing arrowhead, as shown here on the right. In the **Security Centre** as shown above, click the upward pointing arrowhead to collapse each security feature.

The Windows Firewall

The firewall in Windows is a piece of software designed to protect your computer from criminal activity such as hackers or fraudsters. Windows has its own firewall which should be turned on, unless you have installed an Internet security package such as Norton, F-Secure or McAfee.

Turning Windows Firewall On

Select **Start**, **Control Panel**, then double-click **Windows Firewall** and click **Change settings**. If necessary click the circular radio button to make sure **Windows Firewall** is **On**.

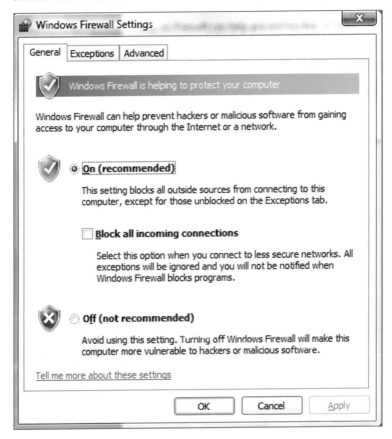

Automatic Updating

Windows Update provides regular modifications to the Windows operating system; these are often designed to make the system more secure and take the form of small pieces of software or "patches". **Windows Update** allows you to schedule your computer to check for the latest updates and download them to your computer from the Internet. Sometimes completely new versions of a major Windows component such as the **Windows Media Player** may be available as an update.

Windows Update can be launched initially from the **Start** menu, then **All Programs** and **Widows Update**. The next time you want to use **Windows Update** it can be launched directly from the **Start** menu. As shown below, the **Windows Update** screen opens and displays the update status of your computer.

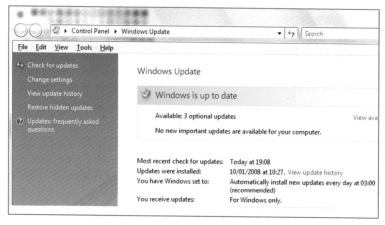

As shown above, you are informed when **Windows Update** last checked for available updates and the date when updates were actually installed. Clicking **Check for updates** above on the left-hand side allows you to carry out an immediate, unscheduled check for available updates.

Malware Protection

Malware is an abbreviation for malicious software and refers to computer viruses and other malevolent programs; the computer virus is a small program written for the purpose of causing damage and inconvenience. In the worst case it might cause the contents of a hard disc to be wiped.

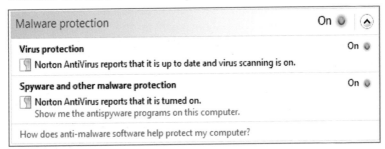

The **Malware protection** extract from the **Windows Security Center** shown above reports on any anti-virus software installed on your computer. It's essential that you have an anti-virus program installed and that this is regularly updated so that it can detect and deal with the latest viruses.

Well known anti-virus software includes Norton AntiVirus, McAfee VirusScan, F-Secure Anti-Virus and AVG Anti-Virus. Many companies also produce complete Internet security packages which include anti-virus software as well as firewalls and protection against *spyware* – software designed to collect personal information from a computer.

Anti-virus/Internet Security packages typically costs £20 – £50 and this includes the software CD/DVD and a year's updates of virus definitions. Updates are normally downloaded automatically from the Internet. Some companies now allow one software package to be legally installed on up to three computers. Subscriptions to an anti-virus package are normally renewed annually.

9

The Anatomy of a Computer

Introduction

This chapter has been left until last because it explains the technical terms, jargon, etc., which many people find off-putting — terms like "RAM", "megabytes", "motherboard" and "dual-core" processor for example. However, it is hoped that the following pages will provide a clear understanding of the functions of the main components common to all computers and serve as a reference section to explain the unavoidable jargon in the rest of the book.

In recent years computers have become much easier to use and are now a popular consumer product, a versatile tool to which many people have access; it's no longer essential to be a technical expert to use a laptop or desktop computer. Many people now surf the Internet, send an e-mail or type a report, without any idea of what's happening under the cover of their machine; in much the same way you can drive a car without knowing what's under the bonnet. However, although you may be able to <u>use</u> your computer quite happily, without some understanding of its vital innards you probably won't make the most of your computing activities.

Of course, behind many technically-unaware computer users there is often a computer guru in the background, to be called upon whenever necessary to solve problems or give advice. Perhaps your son, daughter, whiz-kid grandchild or a helpful neighbour acts as your computing lifeline. This is fine unless the computing guru moves away or is no longer available for any reason.

If you depend on someone else to solve your computing problems, think how much better it would be to become more independent and self-reliant. At the same time you would gain self-esteem and, perhaps, respect amongst your friends and family by increasing your own technical prowess.

It's not difficult to understand the basic operation of a computer, provided any jargon is clearly explained in simple language. The next few pages describe the most important components which are present in every computer; these notes are intended to provide a basic knowledge of each component and its function. This should give you a better understanding of your computer and in particular should help you to:

- Make informed choices when buying new equipment.

- Avoid being blinded with science when dealing with "smart alec" sales people.

- Hold your own when talking to computer-literate friends and "geeks" in social situations.

- Astound your children and grandchildren with your new-found expertise.

- Improve your computer's performance by knowing which are the critical components to upgrade.

- Understand technical problems and attempt solutions.

- Save money and avoid being ripped off by unscrupulous computer repairers.

- Gain confidence to join a local computer class.

The next few pages show how you can discover the specification of your own computer and goes on to explain the functions of the key components which are essential to all computers.

Checking the Specification of Your Computer

Click the **Start** button at the bottom left-hand corner of the screen and then click **Control Panel** from the **Start Menu**. The **Control Panel** window opens, displaying a large array of colourful icons, as shown below in **Classic View**. These icons represent tools for carrying out various tasks such as altering settings or displaying information.

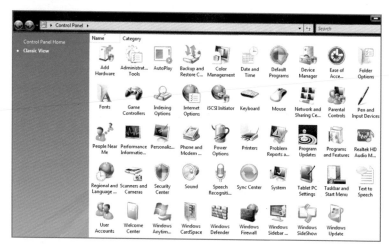

From the lower right of the **Control Panel** window shown in **Classic View** above, double-click the **System** icon. The **System** window opens, revealing information about your computer, as shown below.

System

System	
Rating:	**3.1** Windows Experience Index
Processor:	AMD Athlon(tm) Processor LE-1640 2.60 GHz
Memory (RAM):	1919 MB
System type:	32-bit Operating System

The Processor

This is also known as the CPU or Central Processing Unit. The processor is the "brains" of any computer; the processor itself is an unimpressive-looking flat chip, as shown on the right. Several hundred small pins are used to connect the processor to the *motherboard*, the large circuit board (page 115) into which all the other components are connected.

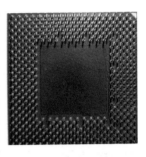

An AMD Athlon processor

The processor executes the programs, i.e. sets of instructions, which tell the computer what to do. A program is temporarily loaded into the computer's memory from the hard disc. (Memory and hard discs are discussed shortly).

Data in a computer is represented in the *binary code* as strings of 0s and 1s (*bits*). The data travels between components inside the computer,

The processor socket on the motherboard

such as the memory and the processor, along parallel wires on the motherboard (page 115). These parallel wires are known as the *data highway* or the *data bus,* typically 32 bits or 64 bits wide, for example. The greater the width of the data bus, the faster the computer's performance.

A very simple example of a program would be to fetch, from the memory, two numbers which you had typed in. Then add them together in the processor and transfer the answer to a section of memory used for the screen display.

The processor is the powerhouse of the computer and generates a lot of heat. This heat is dissipated using a metal *heat sink* and a *cooling fan* as shown on the right. These sit on top of the processor. Laptop computers, being much smaller than desktop machines, are designed to run slower so that they generate less heat in their confined space. In addition, laptops also have a small heat sink, fan and pipes designed to dissipate the heat generated by the processor.

Heat sink and fan

Processor Speed in Gigahertz

The processor incorporates a *clock* which generates electronic pulses or cycles. This determines the speed the computer can carry out instructions and move data around.

The speed of the processor is crucial to the way the computer performs; the example at the bottom of page 103 shows that the processor has a speed of 2.60GHz (or Gigahertz). 1GHz is a measure of frequency and means 1,000,000,000 cycles per second.

When Windows Vista was first introduced it was stated that a 1GHz processor was needed to run the new, power-hungry Vista operating system. (Windows Vista is discussed in detail shortly). I use a 1.60GHz Windows Vista computer for general tasks such as typesetting books like this one, creating spreadsheets (financial calculations) and surfing the Internet. The performance of a 1.60GHz processor is quite adequate for this type of work. However, for certain applications, such as complex graphics, multimedia work and the latest games, a more powerful processor may be required. Processor speeds ranging from 1 to 3GHz are typical on new computers at the time of writing.

Speeding Up the Computer

It may be possible to improve the performance of a computer by fitting a faster processor, which must be compatible with the motherboard. The old processor is removed after raising a small lever and the new processor is simply plugged in.

You can speed up a processor by "over-clocking", i.e. increasing the processor clock speed; however, this is not recommended as it may result in overheating and invalidation of the computer's warranty.

The CPU Cache

Many advertisements refer to a computer having a *1MB cache* or perhaps a *4MB or 8MB cache* on a more expensive machine. The CPU cache is extra memory within the CPU itself, used to speed up the computer. Frequently-used data is temporarily stored in the cache since this is quicker than fetching it repeatedly from the main memory, which is further away across the motherboard. (Memory and megabytes (MB) are discussed shortly).

Multi-Core Processors

Some of the latest CPUs have two processor *cores* mounted on a single chip , examples being the Intel Core 2 Duo and the AMD Athlon X2. These *dual core processors* are faster because they are capable of *multi-tasking* (running two or more programs simultaneously). *Triple* and *Quad core* processors are also available, especially for demanding applications requiring great computing power, such as some games, graphics and multi-media work.

Well-known modern processors are the Athlon, Sempron and Turion from AMD (Advanced Micro Devices, Inc) and the Celeron, Pentium and Core 2 Duo made by the Intel Corporation.

Ordinary single core processors can be bought for as little as £30 or less, while the latest multi-core devices may cost several hundred pounds.

The Memory or RAM

One definition of a computer is a machine which can carry out a sequence of stored instructions; these instructions are known as a *program* and they are stored in the computer's memory or RAM (Random Access Memory). The memory can be thought of as millions of small boxes containing data and instructions. The processor moves data in and out of the memory to carry out a particular task. Any data you type in at the keyboard is stored in the memory.

The memory contains:

* The program or software you are currently using, such as an Internet browser, a game or an e-mail program.

* The data for the current program, such as a file of names and addresses, music or the text of a document.

* The computer's operating system, such as Windows XP or Vista, a set of programs responsible for overall control of the computer.

It's important to realise the difference between the RAM, sometimes called the *main memory* , and other forms of storage. The programs and data in the RAM are *temporary*; when you switch the computer off at the end of a session the RAM is emptied. If you've just spent two hours on the computer typing a report or designing a kitchen, for example, the work will be lost unless you record it on some form of *permanent storage*. The latter usually means the computer's internal hard disc or one of the very popular *flash drives* discussed later. Confusion can arise because these forms of permanent storage are also sometimes referred to as memory. Temporary memory in the form of RAM is often defined as *volatile,* while *permanent storage* on magnetic media such as hard discs is *non-volatile* memory.

Memory Modules

Memory or RAM is supplied on modules consisting of a set of chips on a small printed circuit board, as shown below. These are known as *DIMMs* or *Dual In-line Memory Modules*.

A memory module or DIMM

Bits and Bytes — Units of Memory Size

Inside the computer, data and instructions are converted to the *binary code*, where everything is represented by strings of 0s and 1s. So, for example, the letter **A** might be coded as 1000001. The 0s and 1s are known as *binary digits* or *bits* for short. Every letter of the alphabet, number, punctuation mark, keyboard character or program instruction can be represented by groups of bits. These are usually arranged in groups of 8 bits known as a *byte*. As computers have become more powerful over the years, memory sizes have been quoted first in *kilobytes*, then in *megabytes* and nowadays in *gigabytes,* as defined below.

Byte	A group of 8 binary digits (0s and 1s) or bits. A byte may be used to represent a digit 0-9, a letter, punctuation mark or keyboard character, for example.
Kilobyte (K):	1024 bytes
Megabyte (MB):	About 1 million bytes (1,048,576 to be exact).
Gigabyte (GB):	About 1 billion bytes (1,073,741,824 to be exact).

Memory Needed for Windows Vista

The computer specification listed at the bottom of page 103 of this book stated a memory (RAM) size of 1919 MB. Microsoft recommend a minimum RAM of 512MB and preferably at least 1GB, to get the best from the Vista operating system. Most new computers are now delivered with a RAM of at least 1GB with higher performance machines having 2 or 4GB. The latest high performance memory is known as **DDR2 SDRAM** or *double-data-rate two synchronous dynamic random access memory* .

Adding Extra Memory

Increasing the amount of memory can be very rewarding in terms of improved performance and it's a task which anyone can accomplish. We recently added an extra memory module to a laptop which had been abandoned because it ran very slowly. After a few minutes work to fit extra memory costing £20, the speed of the laptop was dramatically increased.

It's usually a simple task to add extra memory and no special technical skill is required. Before buying extra memory you need to check that it's compatible with your particular motherboard. You may be able to increase the memory by adding an extra DIMM in an empty slot on the motherboard or by replacing a module with one of higher capacity.

Before starting work, discharge any static electricity, e.g. by touching a water pipe or by using an anti-static wrist strap. Care should be taken to avoid touching the contacts at the bottom of the DIMM. The DIMM is plugged into a slot in the motherboard and held in place by plastic clips at each end, as shown on page 115. A notch on the bottom of the module engages with a spigot on the motherboard, preventing you from fitting it the wrong way round. If the memory is faulty or incorrectly fitted, the computer will "beep" on starting up.

Prices of memory fluctuate but currently 1GB of DDR2 memory is about £20 and a 2GB module costs around £30.

Checking Your Hard Disc Capacity

Click the **Start** button at the bottom left of the screen to open the **Start Menu**. Now click **Computer** on the **Start Menu** if you are using Windows Vista or click **My Computer** in Windows XP. A window opens, revealing all of the disc resources on your computer, as shown in the extract below.

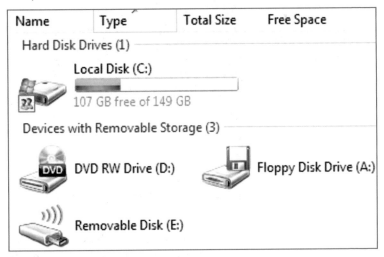

As shown above, the hard disc drive on this particular computer has a total capacity of 149GB. Being a fairly new machine, there is still 107GB free. (Gigabytes (GB) are defined on page 108). The hard disc drive is also known as the hard *disk* drive using American spelling, or more simply the hard drive, the **(C:)** drive or **(D:)** drive if two hard drives are fitted to the computer.

A typical 160GB hard disc would, for example, have the capacity to store over 100,000 photographs, 40,000 music tracks or more than 200 videos. A photo copied straight from a digital camera can easily take up 500KB — 1MB or more on the hard disc.

This chapter, including all the text and images takes up 5.79MB.

The Hard Disc Revealed

You won't normally see your computer's hard disc, although you'll probably hear it, spinning away at several thousand revolutions per minute inside your computer's case.

An internal hard disc drive with the casing removed

Software on the Hard disc

The hard disc is your computer's library where all of your software is saved, recorded permanently on the magnetic surfaces of the disc. When you launch i.e. start a program, it is temporarily copied into the RAM or main memory of the computer, where it's available for use by the processor, as described earlier. The software on the hard disc includes the operating system such as Windows Vista or XP and any programs you've installed, such as Microsoft Office or a photo editing program such as Adobe Photoshop Elements, for example. *Installing software* means copying a program from the manufacturer's CDs or DVDs onto your hard disc.

Modern software requires a lot of hard disc space; Microsoft specify that Windows Vista requires 15GB of free space on the hard disc. Adobe recommend at least 1.5GB of available hard disc space for the popular Photoshop Elements 6 software.

Data on the Hard Disc

The hard disc is the place where all of the work you create is saved. For example, the text of a letter, report or book or all of your digital photographs and favourite music tracks and videos.

Each item that you save on the hard disc is known as a *file*; you give each file a name and a *file name extension* is added automatically. For example, a short story might be saved as **ghostlytale.docx**, with **.docx** indicating a document created in Microsoft Word 2007. A photograph might be saved as **party.jpg**, where **.jpg** is a common photographic file format.

Ideally the data files on your hard disc should be organised into a hierarchy of meaningful categories or *folders*, as shown on the right. This should make it easier to find and retrieve data at a later time. You can create more folders or *sub-folders* within a folder. For example, the **Holidays** folder on the right could be sub-divided into **Portugal**, **Scotland** and **Ireland** for example, to include your photos from different holiday destinations.

Although sometimes referred to as *permanent memory*, the data on the hard disc can easily be deleted, either deliberately or accidentally. It's essential, therefore, to make *backup copies* of important documents or photographs, etc., on a separate medium such as a CD or DVD. The *flash drive* is a simple plug-in form of storage, ideal for making quick copies of files from the hard disc. For larger backups, *external hard disc drives* are available which simply plug into a port or socket on the computer. Hard disc drives of 150 — 500GB are typical on new computers. You can replace your hard disc drive with a larger one (or add a second hard drive) for around £30 — £60 depending on the size.

A flash drive

PATA and SATA Hard Disc Drives

The internal hard disc revolves at high speed, taking its electrical power from one of the multi-coloured cables coming from the computer's power supply unit. Data from the hard disc is transferred to and from the memory via one of two types of cable.

The PATA or IDE Cable

This is an earlier design, a flat ribbon cable about one and a half inches wide, formerly known as IDE and now called PATA. The PATA cable allows two hard  disc drives to be connected on one cable, in what is known as the *master/slave* configuration. The master is the primary drive used when the computer starts up and for subsequent running, while the secondary slave is used for additional storage.

The SATA Cable

This is a newer type of cable, bright red in colour, much less bulky than the PATA cable and designed to give better data transfer speed.

Each SATA drive has its own separate cable and modern motherboards have sockets to connect up to four SATA drives. It's possible to select which SATA drive is used to start or "boot up" the computer.

Formatting a New or Faulty Hard Disc Drive

A new hard disc has to be prepared for use by a process known as *formatting*; this process may also be used to repair a faulty hard disc. Formatting involves *wiping* the entire contents of the hard disc, so that any software and data files are removed. Hence the need to keep your original software CDs and DVDs and to make backup copies of all important data files, so that the contents of the hard disc can be restored to their original state.

Expansion Cards

The graphics components on your computer may be "on-board" i.e. built into the motherboard, the main printed circuit board of the computer shown on the next page; alternatively a separate graphics *expansion card*, as shown below, may be plugged into the motherboard.

An expansion card used to control the display of graphics

To display Windows Vista at its best, you need relatively powerful graphics facilities, compatible with a technical specification known as DirectX 9. The graphics card should also have at least 128MB of built-in memory of its own. The NVIDIA GeForce card shown above has 256MB of on-board memory and fits into a special graphics slot on the motherboard.

The latest type of graphics slot is known as PCI-Express and this superseded the earlier AGP slot. PCI-Express cards are quite different from standard PCI cards and are not interchangeable, so care should be taken when ordering new components. New motherboards are supplied with at least one PCI-Express slot for a graphics card and several empty PCI slots, shown as five whitish vertical rectangles on the next page; these standard PCI slots may be used to add additional facilities such as extra USB ports. It's quite feasible to fit an expansion card yourself — it just pushes into a motherboard slot and is retained by a single screw.

The Motherboard

This is the main circuit board to which every other component of the computer is connected in some way. Some components plug directly into sockets on the motherboard while peripheral devices such as printers and monitors connect via cables.

The motherboard into which all other components are connected

In the motherboard above, the white rectangular area on the middle right is the socket for the processor. On the left-hand side of the socket you can see the lever used to release the processor chip itself. The five white rectangles on the left are the PCI slots for expansion cards, such as a sound card. The brown slot to the right of the five white slots is an AGP slot for a graphics card. The long, blue, rectangular strips near the bottom right of the motherboard are slots for the plug-in memory modules. The white clips which retain the memory modules are visible at each end of the two memory slots.

Data travels between the various components such as the memory and the processor along wires built into the motherboard. These wire "highways" are known as the *data bus*.

Jargon at a Glance

Byte The amount of memory required to store, for example, a letter of the alphabet or a keyboard character.

CPU Cache Special memory, within the processor, used to speed up the computer by keeping frequently-used data in close proximity.

Data Bus The "highway" of fine wires along which data travels.

Dual-core processor Two processor cores on a single chip.

Expansion card A printed circuit board which plugs into a slot in the motherboard, e.g. to better provide graphics or sound facilities.

Formatting A process used to prepare a new hard disc drive or to repair a faulty drive, "wiping" any existing software or data files .

Gigabyte (GB) Approximately 1000 MB.

Gigahertz A measure of the speed of a processor.

Hard Disc Drive A set of high speed magnetic discs on a spindle, used to *permanently* store software and data files. SATA drives are the latest design, succeeding PATA drives, formerly known as IDE.

Kilobyte (K) 1024 bytes.

Megabyte (MB) Unit of measure for memory or hard disc storage capacity. 1 megabyte is approximately 1 million bytes.

Memory (RAM) A module or strip of microchips used to *temporarily* store the programs and data during the current computing session.

Motherboard The large printed circuit board, inside a computer, to which the other components are connected.

Operating system A suite of programs, such as Windows XP or Windows Vista, in overall control of all aspects of the computer.

Processor (CPU) A chip, usually called the "brains" of the computer, used for all calculating, sorting and processing tasks.

Program A set of instructions or commands which enable the computer to perform tasks such as word processing, calculating, drawing or playing music.

Index